CARIBBEAN
potluck

Suzanne & Michelle Rousseau are the official culinary hostesses for the Jamaica Tourist Board, for which they've filmed the "Island Potluck" web series. Former restaurateurs and award-winning caterers who have thrown parties for the Prime Minister of Jamaica, the Prince of Wales, and celebrities like Ewan MacGregor, the sisters are currently filming the first season of their cooking show, "Two Sisters and a Meal." Presently residing in Kingston, Jamaica, both girls have lived and travelled widely in the Caribbean, North America, Europe and Asia. To view their recipes, videos and blogs, visit them at www.2sistersandameal.com.

SUZANNE & MICHELLE ROUSSEAU

CARIBBEAN *potluck*

MODERN RECIPES FROM OUR FAMILY KITCHEN

Photography by Ellen Silverman

Kyle Books

Dedication

To the legacy of our family
For our grandparents, Hugh and Mae,
Hopi and Enid, whose bright spirits have
guided us from beyond during the writing
of this book
For our parents, Peter and Beverly, for
ALWAYS allowing us to be ourselves,
and being our champions through success
and failure

Published in 2014 by Kyle Books
www.kylebooks.com

Distributed by National Book Network
4501 Forbes Blvd., Suite 200
Lanham, MD 20706
Phone: (800) 462-6420
Fax: (800) 338-4550
customercare@nbnbooks.com

10 9 8 7 6 5 4 3 2 1

ISBN: 978-1-909487-09-3

Text © 2014 by Suzanne Rousseau and
Michelle Rousseau
Photography © 2014 by Ellen Silverman
Book design © 2014 by Kyle Cathie Ltd

Project editor Anja Schmidt
Designer Lucy Parissi
Photographer Ellen Silverman
Food styling Christine Albano
Prop styling Marina Malchin
Copyeditor Sarah Scheffel
Proofreader Liana Krissoff
Production by Nic Jones, David Hearn,
and Lisa Pinnell

Library of Congress Control No. 2014930857

Color Reproduction by ALTA London

Printed and bound in China by C&C Offset
Printing Company Ltd.

CONTENTS

FOREWORD

Food is love, nurturing, intimacy, joy and communication; it tells a tale of family, history, culture and tradition.

When Suzanne and Michelle asked me to write the foreword for this first of what I predict to be many publications, I was honored. This is more than just a cookbook. In this work Suzanne and Michelle draw on their background and Caribbean upbringing to create a potpourri of delectable, exquisite and tantalizing modern Caribbean stories.

As the three of us sat on my patio on a balmy summer August evening in Kingston, Jamaica, these two beautiful and interesting sisters, with very different personalities, briefly shared their lives' journeys, the stories of their travels (all of which encompass food) and the integral part that Caribbean cuisine and culture has played throughout the course of their career and lives. This first publication, *Caribbean Potluck*, flows naturally from the varied menu of their talents and love for the Caribbean region.

In *Caribbean Potluck*, I sense the complementary charge of sister souls who invite us into their world to savor the exquisite flavor of their unique blend of "Caribbean-ness." Their food, and the recipes they present in this book, are the perfect combination of Suzanne's succulent and vibrant emotions and Michelle's smooth and delicate sensitivity.

They bring to the table the merging of two unpretentious souls who have come together to fulfill a legacy, create a new path and serve up some delightful recipes on a platter of love.

"Suzie Q" and "Michy Boo," as they are affectionately called by friends and family, are exciting, witty and beautiful daughters of the Caribbean; in this cookbook they invite us to experience, through their own personal stories and those of their ancestors, the beauty and mystery of Caribbean history and culture. I have had the privilege of sharing many a food experience with them so I am particularly delighted by their writings and find myself inspired by their unforgettable journey, even as I drool over their unique culinary creations.

In *Caribbean Potluck*, Suzanne and Michelle share an authentic Caribbean narrative peppered with mouthwatering and exciting recipes. This is not a work to be consumed hurriedly, but instead it should be leisurely imbibed, savored and relished in a truly spiritual manner, in the manner that one would break bread around a table surrounded by family friends and loved ones.

One Love.
Pat Ramsay

TWO SISTERS:
A JAMAICAN FAMILY STORY

We are sisters with very different personalities; we are friends, we are island girls, and we are business partners. Food has been central to both our personal and professional journeys. We never planned to be in the food business—we got here by chance, or perhaps by luck or, perhaps, by destiny.

We are flip sides to the same coin, and people always marvel at our "twin" energy, although we are not actually twins. Suzanne is older, but often thought to be younger because of her louder, more outspoken and lighthearted disposition. Michelle is the baby, but is considered the more serious one: the fringe dweller, the observer, which is not always an accurate perception of Suzie's quirky little sister. When we meet people for the first time, we are often told that we, "Michy Boo" and "Suzie Q," can be quite an outrageous pair—like "balls of fire." We don't know if this is true, but we do know that we get very excited about the people, places and food that we love, and we don't hesitate to share our excitement with anyone willing to listen.

We have many passions in common and take great delight in each other's company: laughing frequently, dancing any chance we get, traveling the world, meeting fabulous people, and waxing poetic about books, movies, art and food. We share the belief that life should be celebrated in every moment to its fullest. We love Jamaica and we love the Caribbean way of life; it is an integral part of who we are. We have always believed in promoting the best of Caribbean living, in spite of the many challenges faced by what many consider a "Third World lifestyle." We consider being born and raised in Jamaica to be one of our greatest gifts; Jamaica is the blood in our veins, the air that we breathe—the heart and soul of who we are.

Our Modern Caribbean Cooking

Traditional Caribbean food is often represented as hearty, heavy, spicy meals; to an extent, that is true. There are many one-pot dishes and stews that require hours of simmering on the stove to tenderize the inexpensive protein that, historically, was often the only kind locally available. Examples of these traditional one-pot dishes are oxtail and broad beans, curry goat and stew peas in Jamaica,

pepperpot in Guyana, oildown in Grenada, and corn soup and pelau in Trinidad. The food we introduce in this book is not limited to traditional dishes—although we do share our contemporary takes on many island classics. During our years operating restaurants and a catering business (and our travels around the globe), we have developed a more modern approach to Caribbean food. Although we are from Jamaica, we call the food we cook Caribbean, as our cooking is influenced by the food traditions of all the Caribbean islands—Trinidad and Tobago, in particular, as

we spent four formative years there as children.

The recipes we present in this book are our original creations. Some are truly traditional, some are modern versions of traditional dishes and some would not be considered traditionally Caribbean at all; we do consider them Caribbean, however, because of our predominant use of Caribbean ingredients, spices and seasonings. Many of the recipes herein were created and served during our years as the proprietors and chefs at Café Bella, Ciao Bella Caterers and Bellefield Great House. We love Mediterranean cooking, and, in many of our menus, we regularly fuse dishes and techniques from the Mediterranean region with typical Caribbean flavors and seasonings. You'll see examples of Caribbean twists on Italian favorites throughout this book.

The essence of our style, which we call Modern Caribbean Cooking, can be broken down into a few basic concepts:

Marinating Meat: Most Caribbean cooks marinate their meats to add flavor and tenderize the meat. We do the same, no matter what cooking technique we are utilizing.

Blending and Balancing Meals: We like to serve a unique blend of savory and sweet at every meal, with a healthy balance of protein, starch and vegetables, and a wide variety of sides as a way of creating layers of flavor and texture in every meal.

Relying on Caribbean Staples: Ingredients like yam, cassava, cornmeal, sweet potatoes, green and ripe plantain, dasheen, green banana, tropical fruits and fresh coconut feature heavily in our recipes, as these are common staples found in almost any Caribbean kitchen.

Enhancing Food with Caribbean Condiments: We often use a variety of salsas, chutneys, pepper sauces and condiments to enhance the island flavor of a meal or a dish.

Taking Advantage of Caribbean Sweeteners (and Rum): Common to all islands, and prevalent in our recipes, is the use of rum, brown sugar, molasses, honey and other sugar cane derivatives in our cooking, baking and beverages. These sweeteners are an inheritance from our past as sugar-producing islands; a nod to our collective past, they also provide flavor and are healthier than the hyper-refined white sugar that's become so prevalent around the world.

You can choose to follow our recipes exactly as we share them, or feel free to make alterations or eliminations based on your palate. Hot pepper is a signature of the cuisine of many islands, particularly Jamaica and Trinidad, and we tend to use Scotch bonnet peppers liberally for flavor and spice in many of the recipes in this book. If you are not a chile pepper lover, feel free to omit these when you try a recipe. We are advocates of invention and creativity, and believe that there are many ways to cook a great dish—the important thing is that you have a good time doing it. This book is a celebration of our cultural heritage and the Caribbean food, flavors and dishes that have influenced our palates and our culinary style over a lifetime.

Caribbean History: Mixing Food and Identity

It is almost impossible to tell a concise, chronological history of the Caribbean as one entity, as it is comprised of such a wide range of territories—each with its own unique historical, social, cultural, racial and political structure that was heavily influenced by the world power that colonized it. And keep in mind that the islands of the Caribbean Sea are not the only territories that make up the Caribbean; the mainland territories of Belize, Suriname, Guyana and French Guiana also form part of the region.

One effective way to celebrate Caribbean identity is through our cuisine, which is influenced not only by our cultural history and our geography, but also by the subtle nuances, complexities and paradoxes that make up daily Caribbean life. In essence—no matter where we come from, or what language we speak—we are far more alike than we are different. Our common identity lies in our oral histories; in childhood experiences and memories; in music, dances, attitudes; in our shared zest for life; and most importantly, in the food: where we eat, how we eat and what we eat.

Throughout the centuries, the Caribbean's warm and welcoming islands have embraced many cultures and races, adopting and adapting the traditions, cuisines and cultural norms of their new residents. From as early as the late fifteenth century, Caribbean food became, and continues to be, an intriguing fusion of different flavors and ingredients inherited from slavery, and from the many migrants who settled in our region over the past five centuries. In the Caribbean of today, we eat many different types of food. While some of these are not indigenous to our region, we always manage to tweak them to suit our palates and lifestyle—and somehow make them ours.

"Our" Foods

As we delved deeper and deeper into the business of cooking and serving Caribbean food we discovered that what we had always considered to be "our" foods were not really "ours" after all, but instead belonged to all peoples of the region. We discovered that the way we prepared our foods—and in particular the "what," "where," "when" and "how" we consumed them—was, in fact, no different from the way this is done in many other islands in the region. This speaks to both the commonality and the diversity of the Caribbean experience and validates the existence of a universal culture that is uniquely Caribbean in its essence. Growing up in the Caribbean was quite a treat; we have never forgotten the joys of a childhood well lived. "Caribbean-ness" dwells in our memories. The daily lilt of voices raised in song, prayer or protest; the perpetual search for the perfect mango that occupied long and lazy summer days; that sweltering summer heat broken only occasionally by the cool Caribbean Sea breeze; the farm animals, goats and cows, that roamed the city streets and often found their way into our backyard; young children in school uniforms, agitating neighborhood dogs; old ladies dressed in their Sunday best under the blazing midday sun en route to church; roadside food, hot and dubious; the pulsing sound of music blasting from cars. This is the rhythm of the Caribbean that dwells in our souls, and we invite you to explore that with us and partake in its beauty and complexity.

A True Caribbean "Mixup and Blenda"

Our family is the perfect example of what we call "the mix-up and blenda" (a Jamaican patois expression meaning "a diverse mixture and blend of things") that is Caribbean history; complete with our own unique blend of African, French, German, Indian, Scottish, Haitian, Cuban and British heritage. The Rousseau side of the family is descendent from one member of the family and his two sons who came to Jamaica in the nineteenth century via Haiti. Our mother's side of the family is more culturally complex. Our maternal grandfather was born in Cuba and came home to Jamaica at age nine; our maternal grandmother was the daughter of a Scottish immigrant.

Our Fondest Childhood Food Memories

Our childhood memories of food are comforting ones, associated with the tastes and smells of the kitchens of those who made up our world: our parents, Peter and Beverly; our beloved grandparents, Manga (Enid), Mama (Mavis) and Gampi (Hugh); and Aunt Winsome, our father's cousin who lived in England and was mother to our favorite playmate, Caroline. Both of our grandmothers were good cooks in their own right, but Manga was the baker and, boy, could she bake! From puddings, to Easter buns, to patties and plantain tarts, she could do it all. We cherish our early childhood memories of Christmastime at her house, making Christmas puddings with her.

Making pudding at Manga's was a big day. Dried fruits that had been soaked in wine and white rum for months were put in a large washbasin with flour, butter, eggs, allspice, vanilla, and nutmeg. Then, as we anxiously awaited the first taste, Manga would sit on a chair and mix, or "rub," the thick batter by hand with a huge wooden spoon. The aroma was mouth-watering as the ingredients blended together. After what seemed like hours, we would pour the batter into metal cake pans to steam the pudding, finally getting to lick the spoon—the best part of the day.

Our maternal grandmother, whom we called Mama, was quite the opposite of Manga. While Manga was large in stature and personality, Mama was petite and fiery. She never hesitated to remind us that her "father was a Scotsman" while rolling her RRRRs, not unlike a Scottish brogue. Mama was known for cooking some of our favorite comfort food—the kind we dreamed about during our university years in Canada. One favorite dish is Mama's cornmeal porridge, which was always seasoned with just the right amounts of nutmeg, vanilla and condensed milk . . . comfort food at its best! All of our holidays at home shared one requirement: lunch at Mama and Gampi's. We sent our menu requests for macaroni and cheese, mince, ackee and salt fish and fried plantains long before we landed at Norman Manley International Airport in Kingston, and Mama never failed to deliver the perfect lunch every time.

Trinidad, or "Trini" to many island people, was home to us from 1977 to 1982. We have a longtime love affair with Trini food, which continues to grow every time we make our annual trek to Carnival and taste something new. Our daily drive from school while living in Trinidad always involved begging Mummy to stop at the corner shop in Maraval for salt prunes (Chinese plums that have been salted and preserved) and pickled pommecythere (June plum, or as the Trinis say it, "POM-SEE-TAY"). The pommecythere always sat in a jar of vinegar and hot pepper on the countertop, just waiting to be eaten. The salt prunes were huge, red and salty. We also loved the red salt prune dust, which you could buy separately—and we often did.

Our food memories of Trinidad are peppered with tastes of pastelles at Christmastime, rotis of every kind, doubles and pelau: a one-pot dish of chicken, pigeon peas and rice cooked down with coconut milk and seasonings—delish! Trini food is always highly spiced and peppery.

Mango chow was a staple snack for us during mango season. Fortunately, our yard had some good Julie mango trees, so we could make mango chow every single day of the season. A pickle of sorts made with green or "turn" (not quite ripe) mangos, cut into thin slivers and marinated with sea salt, pepper, vinegar and hot pepper or pepper sauce, mango chow is the kind of dish that can give you "colic" (Jamaican for upset stomach); but it's also the kind of snack you can't stop eating once you start. We spent many an afternoon picking "not quite ripe" mangos and making chow in the kitchen, then eating it out of a big bowl outside in the yard, barefoot and happy.

Over the years, we have spent time in other Caribbean islands, each different in character and food depending on its colonial heritage. All of the islands have unique, delicious dishes, but a few of our favorites include: nutmeg jam in Grenada; flying fish in Barbados; ti ponche (rum punch) in St. Lucia; griot pork in Haiti; chicharronnes de pollo (local street-side chicken) in the Dominican Republic; conch fritters in the Bahamas; and frijoles (black beans) in Cuba. Not to be overlooked is the wonderfully fresh seafood prepared on every island. Our favorites include fried fish and festival at Kingston's Hellshire Beach and shark and bake at Maracas Beach in Trinidad.

Along the way, we learned to embrace and celebrate everything our Jamaican culture has to offer and to treat every new experience as an opportunity to learn and grow; this has surely kept us on our toes! Jamaican people are full of contradictions, flowery language, enthusiastic responses and many preconceived ideas about the world; they can make you laugh and they can drive you mad, and guess what? We love them! Connecting with the people around us—and the stories of their lives, families and experiences—has greatly influenced this book. We hope you enjoy the cultural melee of recipes as much as we do!

1

CARIBBEAN KITCHEN 101

THE CARIBBEAN PANTRY

DRIED GOODS / GROCERY ITEMS

Coconut Milk, Coconut Flakes (Unsweetened or Sweetened): Coconut milk comes from the grated white meat of a coconut, and is a popular ingredient in Southeast Asia as well as in the Caribbean. You can buy the liquid canned, or the dehydrated unsweetened powder in packets. Shredded coconut or coconut flakes are also available in the baking aisle of any grocery store, sweetened and unsweetened.

Excelsior Water Crackers: These oven-baked, fat-free crackers are delicious and an absolute must-have. They go well with a simple cup of tea, or as a snack with Solomon Gundy (a Jamaican pickled fish pâté), cheese or jam.

Gungo Peas: Originating in eastern India, these are also known as pigeon peas. A dish of rice and gungo peas (for recipe, see page 142) is common in the Caribbean, usually accompanied by a meat dish. Pigeon peas can also be used in soups, and are split to make dahl.

Hard Dough (Hardo) Bread, Plait Bread, Coco Bread: These traditional island breads are great vehicles for spreads like butter and jam, and are ideal for hearty sandwiches. Stuff a Jamaican patty in the middle and you have a favorite lunch item.

Red Peas, Black Beans, Split Peas: These are common beans and peas used to make dishes such as rice and peas, which is a popular element of Sunday dinner. They are especially delicious when simmered in stews, as they absorb the flavors of the seasonings with which they are cooked.

Rice: A wide variety of white and brown rice is used throughout the Caribbean. White rice is a must, however, to accompany a meal of curried goat (for recipe, see page 96), for example.

CANNED / BOTTLED GOODS

Authentic Hot Pepper Sauce (e.g., Matouk's—not Tabasco!): Matouk's and Walkerswood are two firey brands of hot sauce that allow you to feel the heat build and fill up your entire mouth, leaving your lips on fire. Both brands sell a variety of different heat levels and flavors from which to choose.

Browning: This is a natural food coloring comprised of caramel color, vegetable concentrates and seasonings. It is used to give foods a rich, brown and irresistible color but does not have a taste. Used for both savory and sweet dishes, like oxtail or Christmas pudding, browning is found in most Jamaican kitchens but we don't use it in the book.

Canned Ackee: The ackee is Jamaica's national fruit— ackee and saltfish is one of our best-known local dishes. Ackee is creamy and buttery with a mild nutty taste. When raw it has a waxy texture, but canned ackee has a more mushy consistency.

Cassareep: This syrup is made by boiling the juice of the bitter cassava root to the consistency of molasses and flavoring it with spices. Cassareep is produced mostly in Guyana and is the main ingredient in traditional pepperpot, a meat stew (for recipe, see page 103). Traditionally, it was also used to preserve meats for extended periods of time.

Guava Jelly or Jam: This delicious paste is made by extracting the juice from guavas and boiling it with sugar and lime juice to produce a paste, or jelly, when it cools. Sweet and tart to the taste buds, guava jelly is amazing with peanut butter, cheese, toast and fresh banana bread.

Honey: Honey is as sweet as granulated sugar, making it a natural sugar alternative. Flavors vary depending on the nectar of the flower being used by the honey bee. If you can get your hands on some Jamaican honey, use it for these recipes. It is darker, more caramelized, and sweeter.

Hot Pepper Jelly and Papaya, Banana and Mango Chutneys: An ideal way of preserving fruits, banana, papaya and mango chutneys are spicy-sweet additions to any savory meal. Pepper jelly is made by combining hot local peppers (usually Scotch bonnet) with sugar to make a spicy jelly that complements cheese, sandwiches and all kinds of meats. Chutneys are made from a wide variety of fruits that are cooked down with vinegar, sugar, seasonings and spices. Jellies and chutneys are often condiments at any Caribbean table.

Marmalade: A preserve made from boiling the juice and peel of citrus fruits (like lemon, lime, mandarin, oranges and grapefruit) with sugar and water, marmalade is distinguished from jelly, as the fruit peel and rind are incorporated into the preserve, creating a rougher and chunkier texture than that of jam and adding a slightly bitter taste. We love to serve blue cheese with marmalade, which is a very British pairing that we have adopted in the Caribbean.

Molasses: This is the dark, concentrated liquid byproduct of the sugar-cane refining process. It used to be the primary sweetener in the Caribbean islands and elsewhere before refined white sugar was developed. Molasses is found in many stouts, and used in the distillation of rum.

Pickapeppa: Sometimes described as the "Jamaican A-1," Pickapeppa sauce is made from tamarind. It adds sweetness and spice to any meal, and is particularly delicious as an accompaniment to a piping hot Jamaican patty.

DRIED / PICKLED MEATS & SEAFOOD

Salt Beef, Pork, Pig's Tail: An inheritance from our colonial history, when meats of all kinds were salted or cured in order to preserve them for long periods of time without refrigeration, salt beef and pork are still consumed in many of the islands. They add flavor and protein to soups, stews and one-pot dishes like rice and peas or "oil down," a delicious stew made with coconut milk.

Salt Cod: Also known as salt fish, codfish, and bacalao, this is cod that has been preserved by drying after salting. It is a staple in the cuisine of almost all Caribbean islands and can be prepared in a number of ways, like in the Trini-Style Salt Fish and Bake on page 151. Salt cod was a part of the Triangular Trade between Europe, Africa and the Americas. High-quality cod was sold in Europe, but traders sold a lower-end product of poorly cured salt fish called "West India cure" to plantation owners in the Caribbean, who served it as a cheap form of food for the slave population. In exchange, European traders received sugar, molasses, rum, cotton, tobacco and salt.

Other Salted Fish: Like salt fish and salt mackerel, salt herring is commonly consumed in the Caribbean as a breakfast dish where it's sautéed with peppers, onions and tomatoes. It is also often pickled with a combination of vinegar, hot peppers, onions and vegetables and consumed as a snack on water crackers. Salt mackerel is stewed down in coconut milk with vegetables and seasonings in one of Jamaica's most popular breakfast dishes: mackerel rundown. Served with boiled green bananas, this is one dish that is not to be missed!

ISLAND PRODUCE

In this section, we share an extended glossary of common Caribbean fruits and vegetables, all of which we use in our recipes and some of which may be unfamiliar to you. We provide alternative names, information on how they are used and substitutes for many of these items. This will enable you to identify the ingredients you are buying and provide options for alternatives should any of these items not be available.

Ackee: A native to tropical West Africa, this waxy fruit originally came to Jamaica from West Africa on a slave ship—it is often said that many slaves used to wear the seeds as a talisman around their neck for good luck. If you can't locate fresh ackee, canned ackee is a perfectly acceptable substitution. See page 24 on preparing fresh ackee.

Allspice (Pimento): In Jamaica, we call the allspice berry "pimento." It is a prominent flavor in our cuisine that's used in many dishes, either whole or ground, the most famous of which is our infamous spicy jerk, a spice blend/rub that is used on chicken and other meats. In fact, most of the world's supply of allspice/pimento is grown in Jamaica. The allspice or pimento berry has a unique taste—like a blend of nutmeg, cinnamon, black pepper and clove.

Avocado (Pear / Zaboca): The avocado comes in over eighty varieties. In Jamaica, we call it "pear," while in Trinidad, they refer to it as "zaboca." The king of Jamaican avocados, called a Simmons Pear, is very large and has a green skin with a firm and slightly sweet flesh. Jamaican avocados are only available seasonally, and during pear season slices of avocado presented on platters and sprinkled

with sea salt are a staple at most dinner tables. We also love it on an Excelsior water cracker with pickled herring.

Blue Mountain Coffee: Jamaica is famous the world over for its Blue Mountain coffee, which gets its name from the Blue Mountains where the coffee beans are grown. The coffee industry began in 1725, when Sir Nicholas Lawes, the governor of Jamaica, brought seedlings from Martinique and planted them on his estate. Over the last several decades, Blue Mountain coffee has developed a reputation for its excellence, making it one of the most expensive and sought-after coffees in the world.

Callaloo: This leafy, spinachlike vegetable has a distinctively Caribbean origin. Amaranth is the variety of callaloo found in Jamaica. Also referred to as Chinese spinach or Indian kale, amaranth should not be confused with the callaloo found in the eastern Caribbean, which refers to the leaves of the dasheen plant. Some like callaloo soft, while others prefer it crisp; either way, it is often cooked down with onions, garlic, thyme and Scotch bonnet—usually for a hearty breakfast; see page 23 to prepare callaloo. Kale and collard greens are good substitutes.

Chadon Beni (Culantro): Most popularly known as chadon beni in the English Caribbean, this is a prominent flavor in the cuisine of Trinidad and Tobago. It is also known as recaito in Puerto Rican cuisine. Cilantro/coriander is similar in flavor, but chadon beni is a much more resinous herb and thus more intense and potent. Cilantro may be substituted for chadon beni in any dish. See page 46 for a chadon beni oil.

Cho Cho: A member of the squash family, this rough, prickly-skinned, pear-shaped vegetable grows on vines in cool temperatures. Upon slicing it open, you'll find a very pale green and watery interior, with a soft white seed. Known elsewhere as chayote, mirliton or christophene, cho

cho is probably the most widely used vegetable in the Caribbean; each country has its favorite way to prepare it. Zucchini makes a suitable substitute.

Cinnamon: This sweet spice is obtained from the inner bark of trees from the genus Cinnamumum. It is harvested in the rainy season, then dried in curls or ground into powder. In the Caribbean, cinnamon is used to flavor both sweet and savory foods, but is particularly popular in baking, porridges, drinks and sauces.

Cloves: Native to the Maluku islands in Indonesia, cloves are the aromatic dried flower buds of an evergreen tree. Cloves add a unique flavor to marinades, soups, drinks and pastries and pair very well with cinnamon, allspice, citrus and vanilla.

Coconut: A member of the palm family that's native to Malaysia, the coconut tree yields fruit all year long, which helps explain its prominence in Caribbean cuisine. Coconut is edible in both its green and mature forms. Both

the water and the "jelly," or meat, of the green coconut find their way into island drinks, and meat from the mature, or dried, coconut adds taste to desserts. Coconut milk (liquid and powdered) is now widely sold everywhere in cans and packets, but in the Caribbean fresh coconut milk is often used in traditional recipes. We provide a recipe on page 24, if you'd like to try it too.

Cocoa or Cacao: The Maya people of the Yucatan Peninsula are known as being the first to domesticate the cocoa plant. Its seeds are used to make cocoa powder and chocolate. Good ole Jamaican chocolate "tea" is made by grating and boiling fresh cocoa balls with milk or coconut milk, and sweetening the beverage with brown sugar or condensed milk.

Ginger or Ginger Root: This fragrant spice comes from the plant *Zingiber officinale*. Cultivation began in South Asia and has since spread to East Africa and the Caribbean. It is consumed as a delicacy, medicine or spice. Whether added as an a seasoning in a dish, pickled in vinegar or sherry for a snack, or steeped for tea, ginger is very useful for both culinary and healing purposes.

Green Banana: Although similar in appearance to yellow bananas, the green banana's flesh is firm and starchy, rather than soft and sweet. A staple starch for many tropical populations, green bananas make great chips, salads and porridge, or are enjoyed simply boiled. See page 148 to prepare green bananas.

June Plum (Pommecythere): A tropical fruit containing a fibrous and spiky pit, this is known by many names in various regions, including pommecythere in Trinidad and Tobago, Dominica, Guadeloupe and Martinique. This versatile fruit can be enjoyed when ripe or juiced. In its unripened state, it is good for making jellies, jams, pickles and sauces. Substitute June plums in our Mango Chow recipe, page 185, if you like.

Limes: Limes are one of the most important ingredients in Jamaican sauces and marinades, and are used to perk up both sweet and savory dishes. Jamaican limeade, made with brown sugar, is one of the island's most popular drinks and can be found in the fridges of most Jamaican homes. Jamaican limes have a light yellow skin when ripe, though they are often picked green because they go bad rapidly when ripe. You can substitute whatever limes are readily available in the produce section of your grocery store.

Mango: A fleshy stone fruit native to South Asia, mango is now distributed worldwide and has become one of the most cultivated fruits in the tropics. There are hundreds of different varieties and many different types in the islands, all with a slightly different flavor profile, texture and skin, but all sweet and juicy. Some examples of the many varieties of mango in Jamaica alone are Julie, East Indian, Bombay, Hayden, Nelson, Sweetie, Blackie and Number 11 to name a few. You can use whatever mangos you find in the produce section of your local grocery store in the recipes in this book.

Nutmeg: An evergreen tree indigenous to the Banda Islands in the Moluccas (or Spice Islands) of Indonesia, the nutmeg tree is important for two spices derived from the fruit: nutmeg and mace. Nutmeg is the roughly egg-shaped seed of the tree. Grenada is one of the largest exporters of nutmeg and, accordingly, it is called the Spice Island of the Caribbean. Nutmeg is used to flavor many foods, desserts and drinks in the islands and is a defining flavor in all kinds of Jamaican porridge. Grenadians make a unique and delicious nutmeg jam that is a must try.

Ortanique: A cross between a Valencia orange and a tangerine, this citrus fruit was discovered in the parish of Manchester in central Jamaica in the early 1920s. According to Jamaican folklore, it was developed with the help of a pair of lovebirds—one living in an orange tree, the other in a tangerine tree. Extremely sweet, but well balanced with acidity, it also has a strong, rich aroma. See our Baked Ham with Ortanique-Ginger Glaze on page 84. Oranges can be used in lieu of ortanique in any recipe.

Papaya (Pawpaw): "Pawpaw," as Jamaicans call it, is native to the tropics of South America. Orange in color when ripe, with many small seeds, it is mildly sweet when eaten raw, while the green papaya is better in chutney and relishes. Papaya juice is also refreshing; it is often consumed for breakfast topped with a squeeze of fresh lime. See the Ackee Wontons with Papaya Dipping Sauce on page 36.

Passion Fruit: Also known as granadilla, this pleasantly sweet and simultaneously tart fruit is said to have originally come from South America. Two main types, purple and yellow, are widely cultivated in the Caribbean. Inside are sacs with light orange pulpy juice and many small seeds. Passion fruit can be used raw or cooked, as an ingredient in salads, desserts sauces or juices. We also like it in desserts, like the Lemon Passion Fruit Squares on page 172.

Plantain: Technically a banana-family fruit, but generally regarded as a starchy vegetable, plantains are inedible raw; cooked plantains are widely served as appetizers or side dishes. Plantains are used both when green and when ripe, but the ripe plantains are most popular, whether fried, boiled or roasted. The unripe (green) plantain becomes sweeter and less starchy as it ripens, turning yellow. Plantain is eaten widely throughout the entire Caribbean region; each country has its own particular preparation. See page 138 for help to prep plantain.

Pindars (Peanuts): Known by many local names such as earthnuts, groundnuts and monkey nuts, despite its name and appearance, the peanut is not a nut, but rather a legume. In Jamaica, peanuts are freshly roasted by roadside vendors with mobile roasters at stoplights across the island. They are also eaten raw, added to soups and used to make candies like peanut brittle and "pindarcake," sold by locals.

Pineapple: Named for its resemblance to the pinecone, this tropical plant of South America is cultivated from a crown cutting of the fruit, which could flower in twenty to twenty-four months and fruits in the following six months. Pineapples cannot be picked until ripe because their starch does not convert to sugar after picking. Cowboy and Sugar Loaf are the two most-consumed types of pineapple in Jamaica, but you can use any pineapple found in your local grocery store in our recipes. They can be eaten fresh, cooked in chutneys, salsas or other dishes, or as a juice.

Pumpkin: A gourdlike squash with a thick, green or yellow shell, pumpkin is one of the most consumed vegetables in the islands, particularly in Jamaica, as it grows all year around, is nutritious, filling, and adds body to soups, rice dishes and stews. The calabaza pumpkin in the United States is most similar in texture to Jamaican pumpkin, but any starchy squash may be substituted.

Scotch Bonnet Pepper: Fiery and ranging in color from yellow to orange to red, the Scotch bonnet is considered the leading hot pepper in Jamaica, and one of the hottest in the world. They have an incredible flavor and are used to season many types of dishes, and are often found in hot sauces and condiments. Paired with allspice, these peppers are the basis for Jamaica's jerk seasoning. The seeds hold the most intense heat and can be saved for cultivation. We mostly deseed these chiles for the recipes in this book but sometimes leave them in for some serious heat. You can substitute a habañero for a similar level of heat.

Sorrel (Roselle): An annual plant sometimes called flor de Jamaica that originated in West Africa, sorrel produces deep red flowers that are steeped to make a festive drink, also called "sorrel," popular around the Christmas season that includes ginger, cloves, sugar and rum. Sorrel is also used to make chutney and tea.

Sweetsop: Also called sugar apple or custard apple, this fruit is native to the tropical Americas and widely grown in Colombia, El Salvador, India, and the Philippines. Protected by a green, rough and bumpy exterior, sweetsop breaks open easily when ripe, revealing its pulpy white segments with many black seeds.

Sugar Cane: A species of tall grass native to the warm and tropical regions of South Asia, sugar cane has stout, jointed, fibrous stalks that are rich in sugar and measure six to twenty feet tall. All Caribbean sugar, molasses and rum come from sugar cane, which can also be eaten raw or processed to make granulated or brown sugar. The Dutch introduced sugar plantation societies using African slave labor to the Caribbean in 1640. By the end of the seventeenth century, Jamaica had become England's main "Sugar Island" and remained the world's largest sugar exporter until the 1830s, when slavery was abolished and Cuba overtook its neighbor in sugar production.

Sweet Potato: A large, starchy root vegetable, sweet potato is hard when reaped but softens when cooked. Sometimes referred to as "yam" in parts of North America, the sweet potato is very distinct from a genuine yam (see entry below), which is native to Central Africa and Asia. Its skin color varies among yellow, orange, brown and purple, while inside can range from light yellow to orange. It is eaten widely throughout the Caribbean—enjoyed roasted, mashed or fried as chips or fries, and made into a dessert pudding with raisins and spices. See the sweet potato fries on page 55.

Tamarind: The tamarind tree produces fruit in pods that's used in many cuisines around the world. It is fleshy with a sweet and sour taste when eaten straight from the red-brown pod. In the Caribbean, tamarind is used in many savory dishes, as a pickling agent or to make sauces. A popular snack in the Caribbean is tamarind balls, which are coated in granulated sugar, spices and tamarind juice.

Thyme: A member of the mint family, this herb has a woody stem covered by small, green, aromatic leaves. Best cultivated in a hot, sunny location with well-drained soil, it is used widely in the Caribbean, particularly in Jamaican cuisine. Whenever possible, use fresh thyme rather than dried to capture the superior flavor.

Yellow Yam: Brought to the Caribbean from West Africa as a way to feed slaves working on sugar plantations, yellow yam is one of the most widely consumed ground provisions in the local diet. Although the sweet potato is referred to as a "yam" in parts of the United States and Canada, it is not of the same family. True yam is a firmer and more starchy root vegetable that is enjoyed barbecued, roasted, fried and boiled. See recipes on pages 43 and 127.

HOW TO PREP BASIC ISLAND INGREDIENTS

If you're not familiar with some of the island ingredients used in the recipes in this book or are unsure how to prepare them, in this section, we present you with step-by-step descriptions on how to work with some key items. Be sure to check out our online series, "Caribbean Kitchen 101," where we demonstrate these how-to's. The videos can be accessed through our website: 2sistersandameal.com.

HOW TO WORK WITH A SCOTCH BONNET PEPPER

1 Avoid touching your eyes and face when handling the Scotch bonnet.

2 If you just want to add the chile's aroma to your soup or stew, simply add the whole Scotch bonnet to the pot, along with the other vegetables. Just be careful not to burst the Scotch bonnet during cooking by mixing too vigorously; when the Scotch bonnet has softened down be gentle when removing it. If the Scotch bonnet bursts, the seeds will disperse throughout the soup, making it very, very hot.

3 For mild spice, add two to three slices of the Scotch bonnet, seeds removed. Cut the slices from the end without the stalk.

4 To increase the spice, add an additional slice or two of the Scotch bonnet and seeds to taste.

HOW TO CLEAN AND PREP CALLALOO

1 large bunch callaloo yields about 4 cups

1 Cut the stems off the calalloo leaves and strip the leaves from the stalks, if desired. (You can keep the leaves on the stalk, if you like, but when making a quiche, filling or dip, it is best to strip them off).

2 Place the leaves in a medium stainless-steel bowl. Add 1 teaspoon sea salt and toss to coat, then rinse the callaloo with cold water to remove any insects. Finely slice. At this point, the callaloo is ready to be sautéed or steamed. Cook until bright green in color, but don't overcook, as the leaves will turn brown. Note: Callaloo leaves release a lot of water during cooking so use very moderate amounts of fat to sauté and very little water if steaming.

HOW TO PEEL AND PREP CHO CHO (CHAYOTE)

4 cho cho yield about 8 cups cooked cho cho

1 Using a potato peeler, peel the cho cho under running water as it can have a slimy consitstency. Slice in half lengthwise and scoop or cut out the core. Raw peeled cho cho can be cut into cubes, chopped or julienned.

2 Sauté in a little oil or toss with olive oil and herbs and roast in an oven for 35 minutes. Like zucchini, cho cho has a high water content and cooks quickly.

HOW TO PEEL AND PREPARE YELLOW YAM

3 pounds diced yam yields about 6 cups

1 Fill a large bowl with fresh water mixed with 1 tablespoon salt. Place it nearby because yellow yam immediately turns black when peeled.

2 First, rinse the yam well under running water to remove any dirt particles.

3 Peel the yam under running water as it is quite slimy and as it oxidizes, it changes color quickly. Alternatively, rub 1 teaspoon vegetable oil on your palms before peeling to prevent skin irritation. Immediately place the peeled yam in the bowl of salted water until ready to use.

4 Yam can be boiled and eaten whole, roasted or mashed. Just before you plan to cook it, remove the raw yam from the salted water and cut or slice as the recipe instructs.

5 To boil yam, slice it and bring a deep pot of salted water to a boil. Add the yam to the boiling water and cook for about 30 minutes or until tender. Serve warm.

HOW TO PICK AND BOIL ACKEE

1 dozen fresh ackee pods or 4 fresh ackee fruits yield about 1 cup cooked ackee

1 Choose an ackee fruit with open red skin, as this indicates ripeness. Warning: Consuming ackee when the skin is closed can result in severe illness, as certain parts of the ackee are poisonous. Remove the ackee pods by twisting them gently with your fingers from the skin; each ackee should have about three pods. The pods are firm, waxy, and yellow and each has a black seed attached to the top.

2 Remove the seed from each pod by twisting the seed to the right. Using a small knife, remove the red threadlike substance inside the pod and discard; this is the poisonous part. Repeat with the rest of the pods. Leave the pods whole and clean the ackee fruit well under running water.

3 Bring a pot of salted water to a boil and add the ackee pods. (We like to season the salted water with a sprig of fresh thyme, but this is optional.) Boil for 15 to 20 minutes or until the pods become a brighter yellow and soft and buttery in texture but still slightly firm; you don't want to overcook them as they will become very mushy and difficult to work with.

4 At this point, the ackee is ready to be used in one of our recipes; this is the stage it is in when you buy canned ackee. Use immediately or freeze in a resealable plastic bag for up to 1 week.

HOW TO PICK AND BOIL SALT FISH

1 pound salt cod with bones yields about 2 cups ready-to-cook salt fish

1 Soak the salt cod in fresh water for about 1 hour.

2 In a large pot over high heat, bring enough fresh water to cover the cod to a boil. Add the cod and boil for about 35 minutes, until the flesh of the fish flakes easily when picked. Taste a small piece of the fish and if it still seems too salty, change the water and boil for another 20 minutes. Drain and transfer the fish to a cutting board.

3 If the fish has bones and skin, scrape the skin from the back of the fish with a knife and discard. Using your fingers, pick through the fish and discard the bones. There are many small bones, so this can be a laborious process, but we are always meticulous about picking out as many as we can. Flake the flesh into medium flakes—make sure the flakes are not too small or crumbly in appearance. (De-boned and de-skinned salt cod is available in many markets; simply boil and flake it as described above). At this point, the fish is ready to be used in a recipe as is or marinated and cooked some more.

HOW TO MAKE FRESH COCONUT MILK

1 dry coconut yields 2½ to 3 cups coconut milk

1 Crack open the dried coconut with a hammer. Using a small knife, remove the hard coconut meat that is attached to the pieces of shell.

2 Chop or grate the coconut meat and place in a blender. Add 3 cups water and puree thoroughly.

3 Strain the liquid through a fine-mesh sieve, pressing down on the remaining pulp with the back of a spoon until all the remaining liquid has been extracted and the pulp is dry. Use the coconut milk immediately or freeze in an airtight container for up to 4 weeks. Alternatively, you can buy already frozen coconut milk and just throw it into a dish frozen.

FRESH COCONUT WATER

1 fresh coconut yields 2½ to 3 cups coconut water

1 Start by picking the coconut that's just for you—do you prefer more water, softer meat or just enough water with a thicker, white meat? Younger, greener coconuts tend to have less water and more of the thick, white "jelly" you eat after drinking. The water tends to get sweeter as the coconut gets older, identified by a browner outer husk. You can also shake the nut and listen to gauge the amount of liquid inside.

2 Place the coconut firmly on a sturdy chopping surface— preferably outdoors. Hold one end (keeping your fingers clear of the end you'll be chopping!) and, using a sharp machete or large knife, chop away at the husk at the other end until the inner shell is exposed, leaving a large enough hole to drink or pour the water.

3 You can now drink the water straight from the coconut using a straw, or pour coconut water into a container and store in the refrigerator.

4 To get the meat inside, cut the coconut in half along the grain with the machete. Scrape the coconut jelly, or meat, away from the shell using a piece of the husk as a spoon or using an everyday spoon from the kitchen.

FETIN' TIME

LIGHT SOUPS AND SNACKS

Our time living in Trinidad in the 1970s was defined by what the Trinis call "fetin' and limin'" (that's Trini speak for partying and socializing). Our parents loved to entertain and our household became known for hosting the sweetest fetes around town. We have many a fond memory of our mother rustling up quick but irresistible eats in the kitchen while our dad served his signature cocktails to the guests. Everyone knew that the "pickins and sippins" at our house would be tasty—and always abundant.

Fetin' is a quintessential element of Caribbean living. If you have yet to experience the bacchanal of a Trini soca fete, the raw vibes and pounding bass of a Jamaican street dance, or the decadence of a Carnival mass, then we hope that you'll have the chance to visit our islands and join the party soon. No matter what the occasion, the goal is the same—to laugh, eat, drink, dance, sweat and share in the celebration of life with friends and family.

But, in the islands, it is common for friends or family to just drop in unannounced for a drink and a last-minute lime, or party. Ultimately, we don't need a reason to entertain—and neither do you. So, in this chapter, we've provided recipes for pickins and sippins that are all perfect for impromptu parties. Many of these party snacks can be made ahead, while others are quick to throw together. All are guaranteed to keep you and your guests happy.

GOURMET COCKTAIL PATTIES (PASTELITOS)

In the 1930s, our great-grandmother, Martha Mathilda Briggs, was a commercial baker well known across the island for her Jamaican beef patties, Briggs Patties. Ma Briggs was born in Cuba, and the basis for the infamous patty recipe that she brought to Jamaica could have been the pastel. This light Spanish pastry is traditionally filled with picadillo—cooked-down ground beef that often includes raisins and olives—and has clear similarities to the modern-day Jamaican beef patty. Here, we share some unique new filling recipes that bring a bit of modern Caribbean flavor to pastelitos: a Trini-style chicken with raisins, capers, and olives; curried pumpkin; beef chutney; and cheese and creole lobster. If you can't be bothered to prepare fresh dough, you can use readymade puff pastry. Phyllo dough also makes for an interesting version of these party snacks.

Makes 18 to 20 (4-inch) patties

1 pound all-purpose flour
1 teaspoon sea salt
½ pound cold unsalted butter (2 sticks), cut into ½-inch pieces
¼ cup ice cold water
Filling of choice (recipes follow)
1 egg whisked with 1 tablespoon water

Method

1 Using a fine-mesh sieve, sift together the flour and the salt into a large bowl. With your hands, gently rub the butter into the flour mixture until the mixture achieves a sandy texture. Add the water all at once and mix just until the flour is incorporated and the dough forms a mass. Wrap the dough in plastic and chill in the refrigerator overnight. Remove 1 hour before use to let the dough come to room temperature.

2 Prepare your filling of choice. (Alternatively, you can make the filling up to 2 days ahead and refrigerate.)

3 Preheat the oven to 375°F. Divide the dough into four portions. Roll out each portion ⅛-inch thick and cut into 4-inch circles, creating as little waste as possible. Leftover dough may be tightly wrapped in plastic and frozen for up to 2 weeks.

4 Fill each circle of pastry with about 1 tablespoon filling (if you're making Beef Chutney and Cheese Patties, see Note, page 30), then fold the pastry in half and crimp the edges with a fork to seal. Score the top of each pastry and brush with the egg wash. Bake for 30 to 35 minutes or until the tops are golden brown.

CURRIED PUMPKIN FILLING

Makes 12 patties

1 tablespoon vegetable oil
¼ cup finely chopped onions
¼ cup finely chopped scallions
2 cloves garlic, chopped
1 teaspoon peeled, minced fresh ginger
½ Scotch bonnet, seeded and minced
1 tablespoon curry powder or ground turmeric
2 cups cubed pumpkin, preferably calabaza
1 handful fresh cilantro leaves, chopped
½ pack coconut milk powder mixed with ½ cup water (or ½ cup canned coconut milk)
sea salt and freshly ground black pepper

Method

1 Warm the oil in a large sauté pan over medium heat. Sauté the onions, scallion, garlic and ginger. When the onions are wilted, stir in the Scotch bonnet and curry powder and cook for a 2 to 3 minutes until aromatic.

2 Add the cubed pumpkin and cilantro, quickly toss with the onion mixture, then pour in the coconut milk; simmer for 2 to 3 minutes. Season with salt and pepper. Smash the pumpkin mixture with a potato masher and let cool before filling the patties.

TRINI-STYLE CHICKEN FILLING

Makes 12 patties

3 cloves garlic, chopped
1 tablespoon chopped fresh thyme
½ Scotch bonnet, seeded and minced
sea salt and freshly ground black pepper
1 tablespoon olive oil
1 (8-ounce) boneless, skinless chicken breast
2 tablespoons vegetable oil
½ small yellow onion, chopped
¼ red pepper, chopped
1 tomato, seeded and diced
2 teaspoons tomato paste
1 teaspoon ground paprika
¼ cup raisins
1 tablespoon sliced green olives
2 teaspoons capers, rinsed and drained
1 handful fresh cilantro leaves, chopped
1 teaspoon soy sauce

Method

1 In a baking dish or resealable plastic bag, combine 1 teaspoon garlic, the thyme, Scotch bonnet, a pinch of salt, a grind of fresh pepper and the olive oil. Add the chicken and marinate in the refrigerator for about 2 hours. Remove the chicken breast from the marinade and dice it into very small pieces; set aside.

2 Warm the vegetable oil in a large sauté pan over medium heat. Sauté the onion, red pepper, tomato and the remaining garlic. Add the cubed chicken and sauté until cooked through, 5 to 8 minutes. Add the tomato paste and paprika and cook for about 1 minute, then add the raisins, olives, capers and cilantro. Mix well, sprinkle with the soy sauce, and mix again until well combined. Let cool before filling the patties.

BEEF CHUTNEY AND CHEESE FILLING

Makes 12 patties

4 tablespoons olive oil
3 tablespoons finely chopped yellow onion
3 tablespoons finely chopped scallion
1 teaspoon chopped garlic,
plus 4 whole cloves
2 tablespoons chopped fresh thyme,
plus 2 sprigs
2 tablespoons plus 2 teaspoons soy sauce
6 ounces ground beef
1 tablespoon chopped bell pepper
½ Scotch bonnet, seeded and minced
sea salt and freshly ground black pepper
4 ounces good melting cheese, sliced (like
Provolone, Gruyère or goat cheese)
¼ cup papaya, banana or mango chutney

Method

1 In a baking dish or resealable plastic bag, combine 2 tablespoons of the oil, 1 tablespoon of the onion, 2 tablespoons of the scallion, the chopped garlic, chopped thyme and 2 tablespoons soy sauce. Add the ground beef and marinate for 15 to 20 minutes.

2 To make the filling, heat the remaining 2 tablespoons oil in a large skillet and sauté the whole garlic cloves, the remaining 2 tablespoons onion, 1 tablespoon scallion, bell pepper, and Scotch bonnet for 2 to 3 minutes. Add the beef to the vegetables and sauté until browned, about 5 minutes. Add the sprigs of thyme and 2 teaspoons soy sauce and mix to combine. Season well with salt and pepper. Let cool before filling the patties (see Note).

Note: You'll fill each patty with about 1½ tablespoons beef filling, a small piece of cheese and a dab of chutney.

LOBSTER CREOLE FILLING

Makes 12 patties

1½ teaspoons olive oil
1½ cloves garlic, finely chopped
juice of 1 lime (about 1 tablespoon)
sea salt and freshly ground black pepper
1 teaspoon chili powder
¼ Scotch bonnet, seeded and minced
1½ teaspoons chopped fresh thyme,
plus 2 sprigs
8 ounces fresh or thawed frozen lobster
meat, chopped
1 tablespoon salted butter
½ stalk scallion, chopped
¼ yellow onion, chopped
2 tablespoons chopped red pepper
1 teaspoon paprika
2 teaspoons tomato paste
¼ cup white wine
¾ cup heavy cream
½ bunch fresh parsley, chopped
¼ cup freshly grated Parmesan cheese

Method

1 In a baking dish or resealable plastic bag, combine the oil, one third of the garlic, the lime juice, ½ teaspoon salt, pepper to taste, ½ teaspoon chili powder, Scotch bonnet and chopped thyme. Add the lobster meat and marinate in the refrigerator for about 1 hour.

2 Melt the butter in a large skillet. Add the scallion, onion, red pepper, sprigs of thyme and the remaining two-thirds of the garlic and sauté until wilted, 2 to 3 minutes. Add the lobster, paprika and remaining ½ teaspoon chili powder and season with salt and pepper. Sauté until the lobster is cooked halfway through, stirring frequently, about 3 minutes. Stir in the tomato paste and cook for another minute. Add the wine and cook until completely evaporated.

3 Add the heavy cream, parsley and cheese and cook until the filling has thickened, about 5 minutes. The sauce should be pink and no longer watery. Let cool before filling the patties.

SEVEN-LAYER DIP WITH PLANTAIN CHIPS

This is what we Jamaicans would call very "moreish"—meaning you just want more and more of it! For Caribbean flair, we add a double dose of plantains—in the corn salsa and for serving. We like Iselitas or Soldanas green plantain chips, but use your brand of choice.

Serves 12

For the Corn and Plantain Salsa
1 (15-ounce) can corn, drained
½ cup tomatoes, peeled, seeded and diced
2 tablespoons olive oil, plus more for drizzling
2 tablespoons fresh basil, chopped
1 clove garlic, chopped
sea salt and freshly ground black pepper
½ cup chopped ripe plantain
2 tablespoons chopped scallions
¼ cup roughly chopped cilantro leaves
2 tablespoons lime juice

For the Tomato Cilantro Salsa
1 cup diced plum tomatoes, without seeds
1 teaspoon minced garlic
3 tablespoons olive oil, or more if needed
2 tablespoons chopped fresh cilantro
sea salt and freshly ground black pepper

For the Chipotle Cream Cheese
2 packages (16 ounces total) cream cheese, at room temperature
1 cup sour cream
½ (15-ounce) can chipotle peppers in adobe
1 bunch fresh cilantro, chopped
sea salt and freshly ground black pepper

8 ounces Cheddar cheese, grated
½ (15-ounce) can black beans
1 (2-ounce) can sliced green or black olives
1 avocado, pitted and sliced
8 ounces feta cheese, crumbled (about 2 cups)
2 stalks scallion, chopped
1 handful fresh cilantro leaves, chopped
green plaintain chips, for serving

Method

1 Preheat the oven to 375°F. Toss the corn and tomatoes in some oil with the basil and garlic. Season with salt and pepper and roast in the oven for about 20 minutes until dry.

2 Meanwhile, combine all of the tomato cilantro salsa ingredients in a small bowl and set aside for the flavors to develop.

3 In a small skillet, sauté the plantains in 1 tablespoon of the oil over medium heat until golden brown. Transfer to a bowl and add the roasted corn and tomatoes, scallions, cilantro leaves and lime juice, and the remaining 1 tablespoon oil. Season with salt and pepper.

4 Place the cream cheese, sour cream and chipotle peppers in a food processor and blend. Add the cilantro and season with salt and pepper.

5 On a 12-inch serving platter with sides, spread the chipotle cream cheese to form the base. Top with the grated Cheddar, followed by the black beans, corn and plantain salsa, tomato cilantro salsa, sliced olives, avocado slices, crumbled feta, scallions and chopped cilantro.

6 Serve with the plantain chips.

CARIBBEAN CROSTINI

Inspired by Italian antipasta platters, these crostini are brushed with a spicy herb oil, then heaped with your choice of topping: smoked marlin ceviche; curried ackee; spiced olives; or tomato, bell pepper and Scotch bonnet chokka. All of these versions have made regular appearances on our cocktail and buffet menus, and they're a great option if you're entertaining at home, too. Feel free to use the toppings on other recipes in this book, like the flatbread on page 51 or the twice-fried pressed green plantains on page 138. The herb oil is great for dipping bread or flavoring pastas, so why not make a big batch?

Serves 12
For the Herb Oil
1 cup extra-virgin olive oil
2 cloves garlic, smashed
½ teaspoon sliced Scotch bonnet
2 sprigs fresh thyme
2 sprigs fresh rosemary (or 1 tablespoon dried)
sea salt and freshly ground black pepper

toppings of your choice (recipes follow)
3 baguettes, sliced on a diagonal
sea salt

Method

1 To make herb oil, combine the oil, garlic, Scotch bonnet, thyme and rosemary. Season with salt and pepper. Set aside for 30 minutes; the longer it sits, the better it will taste so if you're making a big batch, refrigerate for up to 1 week.

2 Meanwhile, make your topping of choice or all three.

3 When you're ready to assemble the crostini, preheat the oven to 350°F. Brush the baguette slices with the herb oil and sprinkle with sea salt. Bake until golden brown and crispy, 8 to 10 minutes. Serve with the assorted toppings.

SPICED OLIVES

Makes 4 cups
¼ cup olive oil
1 tablespoon ground cumin
2 teaspoons minced Scotch bonnet
¼ cup fresh or bottled orange juice
zest of 1 large orange
3 rosemary fresh sprigs
2 bay leaves
2 tablespoons tri-color peppercorns
4 cups mixed olives (niçoise, Kalamata, green), drained and rinsed

Method

In a container with a tightly fitted lid, combine the oil, cumin, Scotch bonnet, orange juice and zest, rosemary, bay leaves and peppercorns and shake well. Add the olives, cover and refrigerate for at least 24 hours before serving or up to 3 weeks.

SMOKED MARLIN CEVICHE

Makes about 1 cup

8 ounces smoked marlin, diced (or substitute any other type of smoked fish)

1 stalk scallion, finely sliced

¼ red or yellow pepper, finely chopped

¼ cucumber, seeded and finely chopped

1 tablespoon finely chopped red onion

2 tablespoons chopped fresh cilantro leaves

3 tablespoons extra-virgin olive oil

2 tablespoons fresh lime juice

sea salt and freshly ground black pepper

¼ teaspoon crushed red pepper flakes or to taste

Method

In a medium bowl, combine the fish, scallion, bell pepper, cucumber, red onion and cilantro. Stir in the oil and lime juice, and season with salt and pepper and add the pepper flakes. Refrigerate for at least 4 hours to allow the flavors to blend.

CURRIED ACKEE TOPPING

Makes about 1 cup

1 tablespoon butter or vegetable oil

4 teaspoons minced garlic

2 tablespoons finely chopped fresh thyme

1 teaspoon finely chopped Scotch bonnet

1 small onion, chopped

2 stalks scallion, chopped

½ red or green pepper, chopped

1 pound ackee, picked and boiled (see page 24), or 1 cup canned ackee

sea salt and freshly ground black pepper

1 teaspoon curry powder

2 tablespoons coconut milk powder or 2 tablespoons coconut milk

3 tablespoons grated Parmesan cheese

Method

In a medium sauté pan, melt the butter and sauté the garlic, thyme, Scotch bonnet, onion, scallions and bell pepper until soft, for 2 to 3 minutes. Add the ackee and sauté for about 1 minute. Season with salt and pepper and add the curry powder and coconut milk powder. Cook for about 5 minutes, stirring occasionally, to allow the flavors to blend. Remove from the heat and fold in the Parmesan.

TOMATO, BELL PEPPER AND SCOTCH BONNET CHOKKA

Makes about 1 cup

1 yellow bell pepper
6 plum tomatoes, quartered
½ red onion, sliced
4 whole cloves garlic
½ Scotch bonnet, sliced
12 sprigs fresh thyme
4 tablespoons extra-virgin olive oil
2 tablespoons chopped fresh basil
2 tablespoons chopped fresh cilantro
sea salt and freshly ground black pepper
1 to 2 teaspoons balsamic vinegar, or to taste
4 ounces feta or soft goat cheese, crumbled, for garnish

Method

1 Roast the yellow pepper over an open flame on the stovetop, rotating to get all sides, until the skin is charred but not burnt, about 10 minutes. Cover with plastic wrap and let cool for about 15 minutes. When cool, peel the skin off the pepper; don't rinse it with water, as doing so will remove the flavor. Cut the roasted pepper into strips or large cubes; transfer to a medium bowl and set aside.

2 Preheat the oven to 400°F.

3 In a large bowl, toss the tomatoes, red onion, garlic, Scotch bonnet and thyme with 2 tablespoons of the oil and 1 tablespoon each basil and cilantro. Season with salt and pepper. Transfer to a baking sheet and roast for about 20 minutes until the veggies are slightly caramelized. Let cool before roughly chopping the entire mixture.

4 Add the roasted tomato mixture to the roasted pepper; season with salt and pepper. Add the remaining 2 tablespoons oil, 1 tablespoon each basil and cilantro, and at least 1 teaspoon balsamic vinegar and mix to combine. Sprinkle with the cheese and serve at room temperature.

ACKEE WONTONS WITH PAPAYA DIPPING SAUCE

This is one of our signature dishes: The flavor of the curried ackee filling combined with the Asian-inspired papaya dipping sauce is truly amazing. The wontons can be assembled and frozen ahead of time; that way when you have some impromptu guests, you'll always have something on hand to pop in the fryer for a quick and easy snack.

Makes 48 wontons (serves 12)

2 tablespoons vegetable oil, plus more for deep-frying
½ small yellow onion, finely chopped
3 cloves garlic, minced
1 stalk scallion, finely chopped
1 bunch fresh thyme, chopped
½ bell pepper, chopped
1 teaspoon minced Scotch bonnet
1 tablespoon curry powder
1 bunch fresh cilantro, chopped
1 dozen fresh ackee, picked and boiled (see page 24), or 1 (18-ounce) can ackee
sea salt and freshly ground black pepper
48 wonton wrappers

For the Papaya Dipping Sauce

1 tablespoon dark Asian sesame oil
½ small onion, chopped
1 clove garlic, chopped
1 inch fresh ginger, peeled and chopped
1 bunch fresh thyme
2 cups chopped papaya flesh
1 bunch fresh cilantro, chopped
1 tablespoon distilled white vinegar
2 tablespoons fresh lime juice
1 tablespoon brown sugar
1 tablespoon honey
1 tablespoon Thai sweet chili sauce
1 dash soy sauce

Method

1 In a large sauté pan, warm 2 tablespoons oil over medium heat. Sauté the onion, garlic, scallion, thyme, bell pepper and Scotch bonnet until translucent, about 5 minutes. Add the curry powder and cilantro and cook for about 1 minute until fragrant. Add the ackee and mix well. Season with salt and pepper.

2 To assemble the wontons, work with about 4 wonton wrappers at a time; keep the rest covered with a damp cloth so they don't dry out. Spoon 1 rounded teaspoon filling in the center of each wonton wrapper. With dampened fingers (or a brush), wet the 4 edges of the wrapper and form a triangle by folding the dough in half over the filling, making sure the ends meet and the filling is centered; press down on the edges firmly to seal. Layer the finished wontons between waxed paper and freeze for up to 2 weeks.

3 To make the papaya dipping sauce, warm the sesame oil in a medium skillet over medium heat. Sauté the onion, garlic, ginger and thyme until the onion is wilted and translucent, 2 to 3 minutes. Add the papaya and cilantro and cook for about 5 minutes, until the papaya is tender. Add the vinegar, lime juice, brown sugar, honey, sweet chili sauce and soy sauce and simmer for 10 minutes, stirring occasionally. Transfer to a blender and puree until smooth. Transfer to an airtight container and store in the fridge for up to 2 weeks.

4 When ready to deep-fry, heat 2 to 3 inches of vegetable oil in a medium pot over medium heat. Remove the wontons from the freezer and carefully drop them, in small batches, into the oil and fry until golden brown and crispy. Serve the wontons hot with the dipping sauce alongside.

SPICY BLACK BEAN AND CORN WONTONS WITH PAPAYA DIPPING SAUCE

These little dumplings meld Asian flavors like dark sesame oil and sweet chili garlic sauce with traditional Tex-Mex ingredients like black beans, corn, fresh cilantro, and chili powder. Our papaya dipping sauce on the previous page is a perfect match for these wontons as well.

Makes 36 wontons (serves 12)

2 tablespoons dark Asian sesame oil
½ bell pepper, chopped
1 stalk scallion, diced
½ medium red onion, diced
2 cloves garlic, diced
1 tablespoon chili powder
½ (15-ounce) can corn
½ (15-ounce) can black beans
1 bunch fresh cilantro, chopped
sea salt and freshly ground black pepper
1 teaspoon Thai sweet chili sauce
1 teaspoon rice wine vinegar
36 wonton wrappers
Papaya Dipping Sauce (recipe at left)

Method

1 Heat the sesame oil in a medium saucepan. Add the bell pepper, scallion, red onion, garlic and chili powder and sauté for about 5 minutes, stirring frequently. Add the corn, black beans and cilantro and stir until warmed. Season with salt and pepper.

2 Remove from the heat and mix in the sweet chili sauce and rice vinegar. Assemble the wontons using 1 teaspoon filling, as described in step 2 of the recipe at left. Fry the wontons as instructed in step 4. Serve with the papaya dipping sauce.

JERKED CHICKEN AND CASHEW SPRING ROLLS WITH PEANUT COCONUT DIPPING SAUCE

Building on the "jam Asian" vibe, spring rolls are filled with classic Caribbean jerked chicken complemented by cashews and a tasty array of Asian seasonings. The sweet peanut coconut dipping sauce adds body, and balances the intensity of the spicy jerk seasoning.

Makes 24 small or 12 large spring rolls

12 ounces boneless skinless chicken breast, finely chopped
1½ tablespoons jerk seasoning, preferably Spur Tree or Walker's Wood brand
2 teaspoons honey
1 tablespoon dark Asian sesame oil
1 teaspoon, peeled, finely chopped fresh ginger
⅓ cup cashews, toasted
1 tablespoon oyster sauce
2 stalks scallion, sliced
1 bunch fresh cilantro, chopped
sea salt and freshly ground black pepper
24 small or 12 large spring roll wrappers
1 large egg, whisked with 2 tablespoons water
2 cups vegetable oil, for frying

For the Peanut Coconut Dipping Sauce
(MAKES ABOUT ¾ CUP)
2 tablespoons hot water (or more as needed)
¼ cup chunky peanut butter
¼ cup canned or fresh coconut milk
1 tablespoon fresh lime juice
1 tablespoon brown sugar
1 teaspoon Thai sweet chili sauce
2 teaspoons tamari
2 tablespoons raw cashews
2 teaspoons chopped fresh cilantro
1 tablespoon finely sliced scallion

Method

1 In a large bowl, combine the chicken with the jerk seasoning and 1 teaspoon of the honey, tossing to coat.

2 In a medium skillet, warm the sesame oil over medium heat. Sauté the chicken for 5 minutes. Add the ginger. When the chicken is fully cooked, add the cashews, oyster sauce and the remaining 1 teaspoon honey. Cook until the chicken is browned, about 3 minutes, then stir in the scallions and cilantro. Season with salt and pepper; let cool.

3 To roll the spring rolls, brush both sides of one wrap with the egg wash. Place 2 tablespoons filling at one end of the wrapper. Fold in the sides, roll the spring roll and seal by brushing the loose end with a little egg wash. Repeat with the remaining wrappers and filling. (If not serving right away, layer the spring rolls in an airtight container with waxed paper between the layers. Freeze for up to 2 weeks.)

4 To make the peanut coconut dipping sauce, whisk together the hot water and peanut butter in a bowl until smooth. Add the coconut milk, lime juice, brown sugar, sweet chili sauce and tamari, and whisk until combined. (This sauce should have a dressinglike consistency, so add a little more coconut milk or water if necessary.) In a small sauté pan, toast the cashews until slightly charred, then roughly chop. Add the cashews to the peanut sauce along with the cilantro and scallion and mix well.

5 When ready to serve, heat the vegetable oil in a large pot and fry the spring rolls until golden brown and crispy. Transfer to a paper towel–lined platter. Serve with the peanut dipping sauce.

CALLALOO DIP WITH HOMEMADE ROOT CHIPS

What can we say about this dish except that it is blow-your-mind delicious? Our version of spinach and artichoke dip, the callaloo is intense and flavorful and provides creamy richness, but in a pinch you can substitute kale or collard greens. For dipping, we give a recipe for homemade root vegetable chips made from a mixture of sweet potato, green plantain and dasheen (also known as taro), but store-bought sweet potato, tortilla or pita chips make great substitutions. This veggie puree also works well as a side dish.

Serves 12

4 tablespoons coconut oil
2 stalks scallion, chopped
8 cloves garlic, minced
1 medium yellow onion, diced
1 Scotch bonnet, seeded and minced
1 bunch fresh thyme, chopped
1 bunch fresh callaloo, thinly sliced
(about 5½ cups)
sea salt and freshly ground black pepper
2 cups heavy cream
1 cup grated Parmesan cheese
½ cup panko (Japanese) breadcrumbs

For the Root Chips

2 pounds sweet potato, peeled
2 pounds dasheen or taro, peeled
2 pounds green plantain, peeled
4 cups vegetable oil
sea salt and freshly ground black pepper

Method

1 Preheat the oven to 350°F.

2 Heat 2 tablespoons of the coconut oil in a large skillet over medium heat. Sauté half the scallions, garlic, onion, Scotch bonnet and thyme until softened. Add the callaloo and cook until wilted. Season with salt and pepper.

3 Heat the remaining 2 tablespoons oil in a medium saucepan. Sauté the remaining scallions, garlic, onion, Scotch bonnet and thyme. Stir in the heavy cream, bring to a simmer, then reduce the heat and simmer for about 10 minutes, until the cream is slightly thickened. Stir in ½ cup Parmesan and turn off the heat. Season with salt and pepper, then add the cream sauce to the callaloo mixture.

4 In a small bowl, combine the remaining ½ cup cheese with the breadcrumbs. Pour the callaloo mixture into an ovenproof baking dish, sprinkle with the Parmesan-panko mixture and bake for about 30 minutes, or until the top is golden brown.

5 Meanwhile, thinly slice the root vegetables lengthwise on a mandoline and keep in a bowl of ice water until ready to fry.

6 Heat the vegetable oil in a large frying pan over medium-high heat. Working in batches, take the sliced roots and pat dry. Slip into the frying pan, taking care not to overcrowd the pan, and deep-fry for 3 to 5 minutes, until crispy and golden. Transfer to a tray lined with paper towels to drain. Season with salt and pepper and keep warm. Continue deep-frying until you've gotten through all the root vegetables.

7 Remove the dip from the oven and serve immediately with the root chips.

CHO CHO ZUCCHINI-AND-MINT GAZPACHO

This soup is a refreshingly light change of pace from the typical hearty Jamaican soup. It's cool and clean-tasting—perfect on a hot summer day. Also known as chayote and very similar to zucchini, cho cho is used often in Caribbean cuisine. If you can't find chayote, butternut squash is a nice substitute here.

Serves 8

¼ pound (1 stick) salted butter
2 medium yellow onions, chopped
6 cho chos (chayote), peeled and roughly chopped (about 2½ pounds)
3 zucchinis, roughly chopped (about 2½ pounds)
¼ cup all-purpose flour
½ cup chopped fresh mint leaves (or 3 teaspoons dried), plus fresh leaves for garnish
sea salt and freshly ground black pepper
2 quarts warm water
¼ cup chopped fresh cilantro (plus more as needed)
3 tablespoons fresh lime juice (plus more as needed)
sour cream or chopped avocado, for garnish

Method

1 Melt the butter in a medium saucepan over medium heat. Add the onions, cho chos and zucchini, and sauté until the onions are translucent, 2 to 3 minutes. Add the flour and sauté, stirring constantly, until cooked. Add the mint, season with salt and pepper and cook for 5 minutes. Gradually add the warm water, stirring occasionally. When the vegetable mixture comes to a boil, reduce the heat and simmer for 15 to 20 minutes or until the vegetables are thoroughly cooked and the soup has thickened.

2 Transfer to a blender in batches and puree. Return the puree to the pan over medium heat. Stir in the cilantro and lime juice, then taste and adjust the seasoning, adding more salt, pepper, cilantro and lime juice as needed.

3 Transfer the soup to a stainless-steel bowl set in an ice bath and whisk until cooled. Refrigerate for at least 3 hours, until the gazpacho is properly chilled. Serve garnished with a fresh mint leaf and a swirl of sour cream or chopped avocado.

ROASTED PEPPER AND PUMPKIN SOUP

The smoky sweetness from roasting pumpkin and bell peppers gives this soup great depth of flavor and is delicious! The calabaza pumpkin is most similar to the Jamaican, but any starchy squash can be used.

Serves 8

4 large red peppers
2 pounds peeled pumpkin, roughly chopped
2 small yellow onions, roughly chopped
2 heads scallion, chopped
8 cloves garlic
1 bunch fresh thyme
½ Scotch bonnet, seeded and sliced
¼ cup olive oil
sea salt and freshly ground black pepper
1 (14-ounce) can coconut milk
2 cups vegetable stock or water (plus more as needed)

Method

1 Preheat the oven to 400°F. Meanwhile, roast the red peppers over an open flame on the stovetop until the skin is charred. Wrap in plastic for 15 minutes, then peel and remove the seeds. Set aside.

2 In a large bowl, toss the pumpkin with the onions, scallions, garlic, thyme, Scotch bonnet and oil. Season with salt and pepper and transfer to a baking sheet. Roast for 20 minutes or until the pumpkin is fully cooked.

3 In a blender, puree the peppers and roasted pumpkin mixture with the coconut milk until smooth. Place in a large pot over medium heat. Add the vegetable stock or water and cook until heated through. Season with salt and pepper. If the soup is too thick, add a little more stock. Serve hot.

CREAMY TOMATO AND SCOTCH BONNET SOUP

This cream of tomato soup is simple and delicious. The coconut milk gives it a slightly sweet flavor that tempers the spice of the Scotch bonnet. If you don't want the soup to be spicy, simply leave out the Scotch bonnet.

Serves 6

1 whole head garlic
3 tablespoons olive oil
24 plum tomatoes
1 medium onion, chopped
1 bunch scallions, chopped
2 bunches fresh thyme
½ Scotch bonnet, seeded and chopped
2 tablespoons tomato paste
1 cup water
sea salt and freshly ground black pepper
¼ cup canned coconut milk
1 teaspoon brown sugar

Method

1 Preheat the oven to 350°F. Slice off the root end of the garlic, place in a small baking dish, drizzle with 1 tablespoon of the oil and roast for 20 minutes, or until the garlic is tender when pierced with a knife.

2 Meanwhile, with a paring knife, cut an X at the top of each tomato. Sink the tomatoes in a pot of boiling water for 3 to 5 minutes, until the skin begins to lift. Remove from the water and let cool. Peel the tomatoes, squeeze out their seeds, and chop, reserving any liquid. Strain the liquid and set it and the tomatoes aside.

3 In a large sauté pan over medium heat, warm the remaining 2 tablespoons oil. Add the onion, scallions, thyme and Scotch bonnet and sauté until softened. Add the tomatoes and cook for 5 minutes. Stir in the tomato paste, water and tomato liquid. Season with salt and pepper and cook for 20 minutes, until the tomatoes break down.

4 Squeeze the garlic from its skin and mash it with a little salt. Add the garlic to the soup, then transfer the soup to a blender and puree until very smooth. Return the soup to the pot over medium heat. Stir in the coconut milk and brown sugar and simmer for about 8 minutes. Season again with salt and pepper and serve.

GINGERED PUMPKIN BISQUE

The ginger gives this soup a nice little kick so it's spicy without too much heat. Although the sweet potato is referred to as a "yam" in parts of the United States and Canada, it is not the same. True yellow yam is a firmer and more starchy root vegetable, so be sure to seek it out at a Caribbean market for this recipe. As with the previous recipe, the Calabaza pumpkin is most similar in texture to the Jamaican pumpkin, but feel free to use whatever starchy squash you have on hand.

Serves 12

1½ pounds pumpkin, peeled and chopped
1 pound yellow yam, peeled and diced
1 stalk scallion, chopped
1 whole Scotch bonnet
½ pound cho chos (chayotes), peeled and chopped
½ pound carrots, peeled and chopped
1 tablespoon fresh thyme leaves
2 inches fresh ginger, peeled and smashed
2 packs coconut milk powder or
2 (15-ounce) cans coconut milk
sea salt and freshly ground black pepper

For the Gingered Cream
1½ inches ginger, peeled and finely grated
¼ cup heavy cream

Method

1 In a large soup pot, combine the pumpkin, yam, scallion, Scotch bonnet, cho chos, carrots, thyme and ginger. Add enough water to cover and bring to a boil over high heat. Reduce the heat and simmer for 45 minutes, taking care not to burst the Scotch bonnet, until the pumpkin is soft and completely cooked through. Remove and discard the Scotch bonnet.

2 Transfer the soup in batches to a blender and puree. Strain the pumpkin puree, then return to the pot over medium heat. Whisk in the coconut milk powder until smooth. Season with salt and pepper. If the soup needs further thickening, allow it to simmer and reduce some more.

3 To make the gingered cream, mix the ginger and heavy cream in a small saucepan and warm over medium heat.

4 Serve the soup hot, garnished with a drizzle of the gingered cream.

THE LADIES' LUNCH

SALADS AND SANDWICHES

Over the years, we have catered many showers, tea parties and brunches, and there is always something really satisfying about eating, drinking and chatting with the ladies in our life. This chapter, filled with salad and sandwich recipes, is dedicated to the beautiful women who have supported, taught and befriended us, and who love to lunch as much as we do. In particular, we pay homage to the doyenne of nouvelle Jamaican cuisine, the late Norma Shirley.

Norma's approach to Jamaican food was groundbreaking and memorable. She was the first woman to bring Jamaican cuisine to the world stage—a real pioneer. Her dishes radiated with flavor and were as bold and full of personality and flair as she was.

When you dined at any of Norma's restaurants, you would be sure to find a beautifully set table and exquisitely styled plates. You would also see her bustling between the kitchen and the front of the house dressed in her signature Caribbean style, with a headband and silver bangles. As young women working in food, we were awed and inspired by her presence and touched by her consistent support and interest in us and in our business. She was a mentor and a teacher, quick to advise us and equally quick to endorse us. Plus, she was authentic, fun, feisty and loved to laugh—our kind of lady.

ISLAND CAPRESE WITH SCOTCH BONNET OIL, CHADON BENI OIL AND HONEY BALSAMIC REDUCTION

We love, love, love insalata caprese, that classic Mediterreanean salad of sliced mozzarella and tomatoes drizzled with a little olive oil and a sprinkling of salt. To kick it up with a little island "flava," we add avocado and Scotch bonnet oil—it's super-simple and super-good! You can store these special oils in the fridge for up to 3 weeks. The Scotch bonnet oil will get hotter as it keeps, so you can strain out the seeds to take out some of the bite!

Serves 4 to 6

For the Scotch Bonnet Oil
(Makes about 1 cup)
1 cup olive oil
4 Scotch bonnets, seeded and chopped
2 teaspoons sea salt

For the Chadon Beni (Culantro) Oil
(Makes about 1 cup)
1 cup olive oil
½ cup fresh chadon beni (culantro) or cilantro leaves
2 tablespoons fresh lime juice
2 teaspoons sea salt

For the Honey Balsamic Reduction
(Makes about 1 cup)
1 cup balsamic vinegar
¼ cup honey
2 tablespoons sugar

3 beefsteak tomatoes, sliced
2 small avocados, sliced
8 ounces fresh mozzarella, preferably buffalo-milk, sliced
2 tablespoons finely sliced fresh basil
sea salt and freshly ground black pepper

Method

1 To make the Scotch bonnet oil, puree the oil, Scotch bonnets and salt in a blender until smooth; set aside.

2 To make the chadon beni oil, puree the oil, chadon beni leaves, lime juice and salt in a blender until smooth; set aside.

3 To make the balsamic reduction, combine the balsamic vinegar, honey and sugar in a small saucepan and bring to a simmer over medium heat. Simmer for about 15 minutes, until reduced and syrupy.

4 On a serving platter, arrange the tomatoes, avocados and mozzarella in overlapping layers. Garnish with the basil and season with a generous amount of salt and pepper. Drizzle with 2 tablespoons of the chadon beni oil, 1 to 2 tablespoons of the Scotch bonnet oil and 1 tablespoon of the honey balsamic reduction. The Scotch bonnet oil is spicy, so use at your own discretion! Serve immediately.

MIXED GREENS WITH PLANTAINS, GOAT CHEESE AND CHERRY TOMATOES

This is, hands down, one of the most popular salads on our catering menus. The combination of ripe plantain with goat cheese and a light citrus vinaigrette is delightful. Give it a try for a light lunch.

Serves 4 to 6

2 tablespoons orange marmalade
¼ cup orange juice
1 teaspoon brown sugar
2 tablespoons vegetable oil
1 to 2 ripe plantains, sliced ¼ inch thick on the diagonal (you should have 18 slices)
6 ounces chèvre (or any soft goat cheese)
½ medium red onion, thickly sliced
2 caps portobello mushrooms, cut into strips
1 tablespoon olive oil
2 teaspoons chopped fresh thyme
sea salt and freshly ground black pepper
6 ounces mixed greens
24 cherry or grape tomatoes, sliced in half

For the Citrus Vinaigrette

(Makes about 1 cup)
juice of 6 oranges (about ¾ cup)
1 teaspoon orange zest
6 tablespoons olive oil
1½ tablespoons distilled white vinegar
1 tablespoon lime juice
1 teaspoon Dijon mustard
½ teaspoon sea salt
1 teaspoon freshly ground black pepper
1 teaspoon sugar

Method

1 Preheat the oven to 375°F.

2 In a small saucepan over medium heat, whisk together the marmalade, orange juice and brown sugar and bring to a boil; reduce the heat and simmer for about 15 minutes or until the sauce thickens a bit.

3 Heat the vegetable oil in a skillet and pan-fry the plantain slices for 5 minutes until golden. Drain on a paper towel. Mound each plantain slice with ½ teaspoon goat cheese, drizzle with the marmalade glaze and arrange on a baking sheet. Set aside.

4 Toss the onion and mushrooms with the olive oil, thyme and salt and pepper. Arrange in a single layer on a second baking sheet. Roast the plantains and onion-mushroom mixture for 20 minutes until the plantains are caramelized and the onion-mushroom mixture is cooked through. Set both baking sheets aside to cool.

5 Meanwhile, make the citrus vinaigrette: In a medium bowl, whisk together the orange juice and zest, oil, vinegar, lime juice, mustard, salt, pepper and sugar until well combined and thickened.

6 Place the greens in a large bowl, season with salt and pepper and toss with the citrus vinaigrette. Divide the dressed greens among 4 to 6 plates. Top with the tomato halves and the roasted onions and mushrooms. Garnish each plate with 3 plantain and goat cheese croutons and serve.

RED, GREEN AND GOLD SALAD WITH TOASTED ALMONDS

When we are in the mood for something healthy, we make this salad—with or without the feta, depending on whether we are on or off cheese that day of the week. It makes a lovely, fresh, light lunch—especially on a hot day. Pickled vegetables are a mainstay in many Jamaican kitchens and kept as an accompaniment for meals. So use as many beets as you'd like for this salad and keep the rest.

Serves 6

For the Pickled Beets

½ cup fresh lime juice
¼ cup distilled white vinegar
2 tablespoons sugar
½ cup olive oil
1 tablespoon chopped garlic
1 tablespoon Dijon mustard
sea salt and freshly ground black pepper
6 small boiled beets, peeled and sliced
1 medium red onion, thinly sliced
1 bunch fresh cilantro, chopped

For the Mango Vinaigrette

(MAKES ABOUT 1 CUP)
½ cup mango puree, preferably fresh
⅓ cup distilled white cane vinegar
2 cloves garlic, diced
1 teaspoon Dijon mustard
1 cup extra-virgin olive oil
sea salt and ground white pepper

8 ounces mixed greens
1 medium mango, sliced
1 (15-ounce) can chickpeas
¼ medium red onion, thinly sliced
½ cucumber, cut into matchsticks
½ red bell pepper, cut into matchsticks
1 medium ripe avocado, sliced
4 ounces feta, crumbled (about 1 cup)
sea salt and freshly ground black pepper
3 tablespoons sliced almonds, toasted

Method

1 To make the marinade for the beets, in a small bowl, whisk together the lime juice, vinegar, sugar, oil, garlic and mustard until blended. Season with salt and pepper. In a medium bowl, combine the beets and onion, pour the dressing over the beet mixture and season again with salt and pepper. Stir in the cilantro and let sit for at least 30 minutes or refrigerate for up to 1 week.

2 To make the mango vinaigrette, in a small bowl, whisk together the mango puree, vinegar, garlic and mustard. Gradually add the oil, whisking steadily until the vinaigrette thickens. Season with salt and white pepper.

3 To assemble the salad, place the greens in a large salad bowl. Add the mango, chickpeas, red onion, cucumber, bell pepper and avocado. Add half the feta and season with salt and pepper. Drizzle with a liberal amount of mango vinaigrette and toss. Top with the beets, toasted almonds and the rest of the feta and serve immediately.

FLATBREAD WITH ARUGULA, PROSCIUTTO, MANGO AND MANCHEGO

The combination of sweet mango and salty prosciutto makes a lovely—and surprising—pairing. If you're pressed for time or just feeling lazy, you can buy readymade flatbread and focus your energy on the toppings.

Serves 8

For the Flatbread Dough
4½ cups all-purpose flour
2 teaspoons sea salt
1 envelope instant yeast
¾ cup warm water
4 tablespoons olive oil
2¾ cups cold water

For the Herb Oil
(Makes 1 cup)
1 cup extra-virgin olive oil
1 tablespoon chopped fresh rosemary
1 tablespoon fresh thyme
1 tablespoon chopped garlic
1 tablespoon chopped fresh basil
sea salt

For the Caramelized Red Onion
2 tablespoons olive oil
1 red onion, thinly sliced
sea salt

sea salt
8 ounces thinly sliced prosciutto
8 ounces shaved Manchego cheese
1 cup thinly sliced mango
4 ounces arugula
freshly ground black pepper
1 tablespoon honey basalmic reduction (page 46), or to taste
8 tablespoons fresh basil leaves, torn

Method

1 To make the flatbread dough, in the bowl of a standing mixer fitted with the dough hook, mix the flour and salt until thoroughly incorporated, about 1 minute. Meanwhile, place the yeast in a small bowl and whisk in the warm water, then 3 tablespoons of the oil. Let the yeast rest until it begins to foam, about 10 minutes, then pour into a well in the center of the flour. Mix the flour and yeast solution until well incorporated. Add the cold water to the flour and mix again, until the dough pulls together in a single, unified mass.

2 Turn the dough out onto a lightly floured surface and begin to knead, working the dough with the heel of your hand. Push outward and pull the inside edge over the top. Repeat the process over and over to create a smooth ball of dough, free of stickiness. This should take 6 to 8 minutes. Brush a clean, stainless-steel bowl with the remaining 1 tablespoon oil and put the ball of dough in the bowl. Cover with a clean cloth and let rise at room temperature until it has doubled in size, about 1 hour.

3 Meanwhile, make the herb oil: In a small bowl, whisk together the oil, rosemary, thyme, basil and garlic. Season with salt and let sit for at least 1 hour to let the flavors develop. (You can also use a blender.)

4 To make the caramelized red onion, heat the oil in a medium sauté pan over low heat, then add the onion and season with a little salt. Cook slowly until the onion is caramelized and slightly sweet, 15 to 20 minutes.

5 Divide the dough into 8 balls. (The balls of dough can be individually wrapped in plastic and frozen for up to 2 months.) With a rolling pin, roll each ball into an oval shape. Brush with herb oil, sprinkle with salt and grill on both sides until marked. Cover each grilled flatbread with prosciutto slices and top with the cheese shavings and mango slices.

6 In a small bowl, season the arugula with salt and pepper, then toss with the honey balsamic reduction and herb oil to taste. Mound the arugula on top of the prosciutto, mango and cheese. Add the caramelized onion and basil and serve immediately.

CAESAR SALAD WITH SOLOMON GUNDY CAESAR VINAIGRETTE AND HARDO CROUTONS

One of our head chefs, Sandy Williams, came up with this innovative and tasty twist on the traditional salad. Essentially, we lighten up the traditional Caesar by removing the egg and adding some favorite Caribbean ingredients. The tart vinaigrette is inspired by Solomon Gundy, a Jamaican spread made from pickled herring that we use instead of the traditional anchovies. For a touch of sweetness, we top the salad with some hardo bread croutons and round it off with shaved Parmesan. You can also add grilled chicken, shrimp or bacon bits.

Serves 6

For the Hardo Bread Croutons

5 slices Jamaican hardo bread (or other firm white bread), cut into ½-inch cubes
¼ cup olive oil
4 sprigs fresh thyme, chopped
1 clove garlic, finely minced
sea salt and freshly ground black pepper

For the Solomon Gundy Vinaigrette

(Makes about 2 cups)
1 cup olive oil
2 tablespoons Solomon Gundy, preferably Walkerswood
juice of 6 small limes (about ¼ cup)
5 tablespoons distilled white vinegar
1 tablespoon extra-strong mustard, like Colman's or Dijon
1 tablespoon brown sugar, plus more as needed
1 tablespoon chopped garlic
1 teaspoon freshly ground black pepper

1 head Romaine lettuce, torn into pieces
4 ounces Parmesan cheese, grated (about 1 cup)
sea salt and freshly ground black pepper

Method

1 To make the croutons, preheat the oven to 400°F. In a large bowl, toss the bread with the oil, thyme and garlic, and season with salt and pepper. Spread out on a baking sheet and bake for 20 to 25 minutes, until the croutons are brown and crispy. Let cool.

2 Meanwhile, to make the vinaigrette, in a medium bowl, whisk together the oil, Solomon Gundy, lime juice, vinegar, mustard, brown sugar, garlic and pepper until well combined (or you can whizz in a blender). Taste and adjust the seasoning, adding more brown sugar if necessary.

3 Place the lettuce in a salad bowl. Add half the cheese and half the croutons. Season with salt and pepper. Toss with some of the dressing to taste—be careful not to overdress, as the dressing is very strong. Top with the remaining croutons and cheese and serve immediately.

PRESSED HAM AND THREE-CHEESE SANDWICHES

This jazzy, sweet and spicy version of a grilled ham and cheese (or a croque monsieur without the béchamel) is a definite winner! Pepper jelly is a well-loved condiment used on cheese, sandwiches and meats throughout the Caribbean. It is a spicy but sweet jelly made from hot peppers.

Makes 4 sandwiches

1 tablespoon olive oil
2 medium yellow onions, sliced
sea salt
6 ounces fresh baked honey ham or Black Forest ham, thickly sliced
2 teaspoons honey
8 slices Jamaican hardo bread (or other firm white bread)
4 teaspoons Dijon mustard
6 ounces Gruyère cheese, grated or thinly sliced
2 ounces mozzarella, preferably buffalo-milk, grated or thinly sliced
4 teaspoons hot pepper jelly
3 tablespoons butter
4 tablespoons grated Parmesan cheese

Method

1 Turn on the broiler or preheat the oven to 450°F.

2 In a medium sauté pan, warm the oil over medium heat. Add the onions, sprinkle with salt and cook, stirring occasionally, until browned and wilted. Transfer to a plate and set aside.

3 In the same pan, place the ham slices to warm. As it cooks, drizzle the ham with the honey so it becomes sticky and caramelized.

4 Spread 1 slice of bread with 1 teaspoon mustard. Layer one-fourth of the Gruyère on the mustard, top with some onions, one-fourth of the ham and then one-fourth of the mozzarella cheese. Spread 1 teaspoon pepper jelly on a second slice of bread and place it, jelly side down, on the mozzarella. Spread the top of each sandwich with about 1 teaspoon of the butter. Repeat to create 4 sandwiches in all.

5 In a clean nonstick sauté pan, melt about 1 teaspoon butter over medium heat. Place one sandwich, buttered side up, in the pan and press and hold with the back of the spatula as the sandwich cooks. When the bread is nice and caramelized, flip the sandwich over and repeat on the other side. Once the cheese begins to melt and the bread is nice and crispy, transfer to a baking sheet that has been brushed with a little butter. Repeat with more butter and the remaining sandwiches.

6 Top each sandwich with 1 tablespoon Parmesan and broil until the cheese is melted and slightly brown on top. (Depending on the broiler, this could take anywhere from 2 to 8 minutes—so watch carefully!) Cut each sandwich in half and serve immediately.

JERKED HONEY-BACON CHEESEBURGER WITH SWEET POTATO FRIES

Everyone loves a great burger and this one is delicious. The jerk seasoning provides a nice kick of spice, while the bacon and caramelized onions contribute sweetness. We replace mayonnaise with a spicy aïoli, which adds a smooth creaminess to complement the jerk. We like to use coco bread, as it is softer and moister than a standard hamburger bun.

Makes 6 (4-ounce) burgers

1½ pounds ground beef
2 tablespoons jerk seasoning
1 bunch fresh thyme
1 tablespoon olive oil
½ yellow onion, finely minced, plus 2 yellow onions, sliced
1 clove garlic, chopped
¼ teaspoon ground allspice
sea salt and freshly ground black pepper
2 tablespoons vegetable oil, plus more for brushing
1 (4-ounce) package bacon, slices cut in half to fit on burgers
1 teaspoon honey
5 ounces thinly sliced cheese of choice, such as Cheddar or Swiss
5 coco breads or hamburger buns
Lettuce, sliced tomato, and sliced red onion, for garnish
Sweet Potato Fries with Spiced Salt and Spicy Ketchup (recipe at right), for serving

For the Cilantro-Habanero Aïoli
(MAKES ABOUT 1½ CUPS)
1 cup mayonnaise
½ cup sour cream
½ Scotch bonnet, seeded and minced
1 teaspoon orange zest
1 teaspoon lime zest
2 tablespoons lime juice
1 clove garlic, minced
2 tablespoons chopped scallion
3 tablespoons chopped fresh cilantro
sea salt

Method

1 In a large bowl, combine the ground beef with the jerk seasoning, thyme, olive oil, minced onion, garlic and allspice. Season with salt and pepper. Line a baking sheet with waxed paper. Form the ground beef mixture into five 4-ounce patties and place them on the prepared baking sheet.

2 Make the cilantro-habanero aïoli: In a small bowl, stir together the mayonnaise, sour cream, Scotch bonnet, orange and lime zest, lime juice, garlic, scallion and cilantro. Let sit for at least 30 minutes to allow the flavors to meld. Season with salt.

3 Warm the vegetable oil in a sauté pan over low heat. Add the sliced onions and cook until caramelized, 15 to 20 minutes. Transfer the onions to a plate and set aside. Add the bacon to the same pan and cook, turning from time to time. When the bacon is almost cooked, after 7 to 8 minutes, drizzle the honey over the bacon so it gets nice and sticky.

4 Heat a grill or grill pan to medium heat and preheat the oven to 350°F. Place a baking sheet in the oven to warm. Brush the grill with some oil. Add the burgers and cook to desired doneness (3 to 5 minutes per side for medium or medium-well), then remove from the heat before cooked through. Top each burger with the honey bacon, caramelized onions and a slice of cheese and transfer to the warmed baking sheet. Place the burgers in the oven just until the cheese melts.

5 Meanwhile, toast or grill the hamburger buns. Spread both sides of each bun with 1 tablespoon of the cilantro-habanero aïoli. Top one side of each bun with a burger and place on a serving plate. Top the other side of each bun with a piece of lettuce, tomato and red onion and add to the plate. Serve with sweet potato fries and spicy ketchup.

SWEET POTATO FRIES WITH SPICY KETCHUP AND SPICED SALT

For the Spiced Salt
3 tablespoons fine sea salt
1 tablespoon chopped fresh thyme
½ teaspoon ground cumin
½ teaspoon ground allspice

For the Spicy Ketchup
1 cup ketchup
1 tablespoon Pickapeppa sauce
2 teaspoons hot pepper sauce

2 cups vegetable oil
2 large sweet potatoes, very thinly sliced into shoestrings, soaked in salted water

Method

1 To make the spiced salt, in a small bowl toss together the salt, thyme, cumin and allspice. Transfer to a tightly sealed container. The salt will keep for up to 3 months.

2 To make the spicy ketchup, stir together the ketchup, Pickapeppa sauce and hot sauce. Transfer to a tightly sealed container. The ketchup will keep for up to 3 months in the fridge.

3 In a wide-bottomed saucepan, heat the oil over medium heat. To test the oil, drop in 1 sweet potato fry and see if it fries until brown. When the oil is heated enough, add the rest of the sweet potato fries in batches and fry until golden brown, about 10 minutes. Transfer to paper towels to drain, then fry a second time for about 5 minutes. Season with the spiced salt while still hot. Serve with spicy ketchup.

SMOKED MARLIN AND CREAM CHEESE WITH ONION PICKLE À LA CAFÉ BELLA

People used to tell us that they dreamt about this smoked marlin sandwich, which is the original recipe for the first sandwich we ever served. Our café was located just down the road from the Bob Marley Museum, where the Marley family members spent their days. They regularly called us at around eleven thirty, ordering anywhere from seven to twenty marlin sandwiches for lunch, and sent someone to collect them within fifteen minutes. To say that they loved this sandwich would be an understatement!

Makes 4 sandwiches

4 small yellow onions, very thinly sliced
4 tablespoons capers, drained
1 cup distilled white vinegar
¼ cup sugar
1 pound cream cheese, softened at room temperature
1 cup sour cream
1 tablespoon fresh dill or cilantro leaves, chopped, plus more for garnish
sea salt and freshly ground black pepper
8 slices crusty whole-grain bread or baguette
8 ounces smoked marlin (or another smoked fish, such as smoked trout)
4 lime wedges

Method

1 In a small bowl, combine the onions, capers, vinegar and sugar and let sit for at least 1 hour. The pickled onions can be refrigerated for up to 1 week; you can simply keep adding fresh onions to the marinade.

2 In a small bowl, combine the cream cheese, sour cream, dill, and pinches of salt and pepper and mix well with a wooden spoon. (Alternatively, you can blend in a food processor.)

3 Toast the bread and spread 1 tablespoon of the cream cheese blend on each slice. Layer the marlin thinly on top of the cream cheese on all 8 slices. Top with freshly ground black pepper and a squeeze of fresh lime. Serve open-faced, garnished generously with the pickled onions.

SMOKED TURKEY AND BRIE

Our original recipe for this used honey mustard, which we later replaced with a sorrel chutney for a slightly more Caribbean taste. Here we combine the two. If you can't find sorrel chutney, mango will do.

Makes 4 sandwiches

2 tablespoons honey
2 tablespoons Dijon mustard
2 baguettes, cut into 6-inch portions, each portion split open like a book
4 ounces Brie cheese, cut into 4 thick slices
6 ounces good-quality smoked turkey, thinly sliced
sea salt and freshly ground black pepper
½ small yellow onion, thinly sliced
2 beefsteak tomatoes, sliced
4 lettuce leaves
4 tablespoons red wine vinaigrette (page 181)
sorrel or mango chutney, to taste (optional)

Method

1 Preheat the oven to 375°F. In a small bowl, mix the honey and mustard; set aside.

2 Top one side of each baguette portion with one-quarter of the Brie and place on a baking sheet. Lightly toast in the oven until the Brie is melted.

3 Divide the turkey slices on top of the melted Brie, sprinkle with salt and pepper, and drizzle with the honey mustard. Top each sandwich with onion and tomato slices and 1 lettuce leaf and drizzle with the vinaigrette. If using the chutney, spread it on the other side of each portion of bread. Close each sandwich and slice on the diagonal to serve.

SAUTÉED STEAK AND CHEESE SANDWICHES

Mummy used to make this signature sandwich for us with fresh beef tenderloin; the combination of the Pickapeppa sauce with the mayo and onions is to die for!

Makes 4 sandwiches

1 bunch fresh thyme
2 cloves garlic, chopped
1 teaspoon peeled and grated fresh ginger
½ Scotch bonnet, seeded and finely chopped
1 bunch scallions, sliced
2 tablespoons soy sauce
1 teaspoon brown sugar
8 ounces beef tenderloin, cut into strips
3 tablespoons olive oil
2 medium yellow onions, sliced
4 ounces Emmental cheese, thinly sliced
8 slices Jamaican hardo bread (or other firm white bread)
4 tablespoons mayonnaise
4 teaspoons Dijon mustard
4 teaspoons Pickapeppa sauce
4 lettuce leaves (optional)
8 slices tomato (optional)

Method

1 In a bowl, combine the thyme, garlic, ginger, Scotch bonnet, scallions, soy sauce and brown sugar. Add the beef and marinate for 15 minutes.

2 Meanwhile, in a large skillet over medium to high heat, heat 1 tablespoon of the oil. Add the onions, sprinkle with salt and sauté until browned and softened. Transfer to a plate and set aside.

3 Preheat the oven to 375°F. Add another 1 tablespoon oil to the skillet over high heat. Stir-fry the beef in batches (adding the last tablespoon oil in between). When the beef is brown outside and tender inside, after 2 to 3 minutes, remove from the pan—don't overcook!

4 Divide the cheese among 4 slices of bread. Toast all the bread (including the slices with no cheese) in the oven until the cheese is melted.

5 Spread 1 tablespoon of the mayonnaise and 1 teaspoon of the mustard on the non-cheesy slices of bread. Add the beef and onions. Drizzle the beef with 1 teaspoon Pickapeppa sauce, add the lettuce and tomatoes, if using, and cover with the cheesy slices of bread. Cut each sandwich in half and serve immediately.

CALLALOO STRUDEL WITH CREAM CHEESE À LA RED BONES

This dish is an homage to one of our longtime favorite dining spots in Kingston: the Red Bones Blues Café. This dish has been on their menu for as long as the restaurant has been open, and we order it every time we go there! This is our version of it. If you can't find callaloo, you can substitute spinach or kale.

Serves 4 to 6

1 tablespoon olive oil
1 clove garlic, chopped
1 small yellow onion, chopped
½ Scotch bonnet, seeded and diced
1 bunch fresh thyme, chopped
1 stalk scallion, chopped
1 bunch callaloo, finely sliced (about 4 cups)
1 cup ricotta
sea salt and freshly ground black pepper
8 sheets thawed frozen phyllo pastry
½ cup butter, melted
1 (8-ounce) package cream cheese

For the Cream Sauce

1 cup heavy cream
2 tablespoons fresh lime juice
2 tablespoons sliced scallion
sea salt and freshly ground black pepper

Method

1 Preheat the oven to 375°F.

2 Warm the oil in a large skillet over medium heat. Add the garlic, onion, Scotch bonnet, thyme and scallion and cook until soft, stirring occasionally, 2 to 3 minutes. Add the callaloo and cook, stirring occasionally, until it turns bright green, about 3 minutes. Transfer the callaloo mixture to a strainer and squeeze out all the excess water. Set aside to cool, then transfer to a large bowl and mix in the ricotta. Season with salt and pepper.

3 Place one sheet of phyllo pastry on a dry surface (cover the remaining sheets with a damp cloth so they do not dry out). Brush the pastry with the melted butter, starting at the ends, which tend to dry out first. Place another layer of phyllo on top and brush again with butter. Repeat with all 8 sheets.

4 Cut the cream cheese into 4 slices and arrange side by side on the phyllo, about 3 inches from the edge. Top with the callaloo filling. Roll one edge of the phyllo over the callaloo mixture and keep rolling until the phyllo is all rolled up to form a log. Make sure you end with the cream cheese at the bottom of the log, if not, cut away the excess dough. Brush the seam with melted butter to seal.

5 Place the phyllo roll, seam side down, on a greased sheet pan. Using a sharp knife, score the top of the phyllo to make it easier to slice the strudel neatly after baking. Brush the top of the strudel with more melted butter and bake for 25 to 30 minutes, until lightly browned on top.

6 Meanwhile, to make the cream sauce, bring the heavy cream to a boil in a small saucepan over medium heat. Add the lime juice, reduce the heat and simmer until the cream has reduced and thickened, about 15 minutes. Mix in the scallion and season with salt and pepper.

7 To serve, ladle the cream sauce on 4 to 6 heated plates, slice the strudel and place a piece on each plate.

GRILLED SHRIMP SALAD WITH BLACK BEANS, CORN, PLANTAINS AND CILANTRO

Just one word for you: Yummmmmm! Shrimp is a very popular shellfish that is eaten throughout all the Caribbean islands; Jamaicans particulary love shrimp. We always had to find ways to incorporate shrimp into our buffet recipes. This shrimp marinade also makes incredibly tasty grilled shrimp on their own.

Serves 6 to 8

juice of ½ orange
juice of 1 lime
1¼ teaspoons ground cayenne
1 teaspoon chili powder
1½ teaspoons ground cumin
2 cloves garlic, chopped
1 teaspoon peeled, grated fresh ginger
1 tablespoon honey
2 tablespoons olive oil
sea salt and freshly ground black pepper
1 bunch fresh cilantro, chopped, plus
½ cup chopped
1 pound fresh or frozen thawed shrimp
(21 to 25 count), peeled and deveined,
tail left on
2 tablespoons vegetable oil, plus more
as needed
1 small ripe plantain, cut into cubes
(about ¾ cup)
½ red onion, chopped (about ¼ cup)
1 stalk scallion, thinly sliced
½ red pepper, chopped
1 (15-ounce) can black beans
1 cup canned corn
Lime Vinaigrette (page 75)

Method

1 In a food processor or blender, combine the orange and lime juices, 1 teaspoon of the cayenne, the chili powder, 1 teaspoon of the cumin, the garlic, ginger, honey, olive oil, salt and pepper, and bunch of cilantro and blend. Transfer to a baking dish or resealable plastic bag, add the shrimp and marinate in the refrigerator for at least 1 hour.

2 In a large skillet, warm the vegetable oil over medium heat. Add the plantain and sauté until caramelized and cooked through. Transfer to a large bowl and set aside. In the same pan, sauté the onion, scallion and bell pepper for 2 to 3 minutes, then add to the bowl with the plantains.

3 Add a little more oil to the pan and stir-fry the shrimp until opaque. (Alternatively, you can grill the shrimp.)

4 While still warm, add the shrimp to the bowl with the vegetables. Add the black beans, corn, ½ cup cilantro, ½ teaspoon cumin and ¼ teaspoon cayenne. Add the vinaigrette, toss to combine, and season with salt and pepper. Let rest for at least 30 minutes before serving to allow the flavors to develop.

CIAO BELLA

WICKED PASTA, ISLAND STYLE

Three visits to Italy during our teens and early twenties solidified our love affair with La Bella Italia—its culture, people, lifestyle and food. Much comes to mind when we think of Italy: the enthusiasm and zest for life, the crazy driving, the catcalls from the men in the streets, and, of course, the mouthwatering food! We loved Italy so much that we decided to name our business Ciao Bella. We even made the Italian approach to life the basis for our first advertising campaign, using the tagline "Hello, beautiful" to introduce our brand. Beauty is, after all, what Italy is all about: beautiful people, beautiful food, beautiful architecture, beautiful art—there is beauty every place you look!

On one of our early trips to Italy, we formed a relationship with a wonderful Italian family who had ties to Jamaica. They generously offered us hands-on instruction and insights on cooking and eating the Italian way. In their villa outside of Rome and at their grandmother's house in Forte dei Marmi, we cooked pasta, fresh pizza (in their outdoor brick oven), bruschetta and tiramisu. We dined al fresco in their garden, under the stars, and a great and long-lasting friendship developed. We thank the Alfano family for this formidable culinary experience, which has influenced all that we have cooked, both professionally and at home, ever since.

Our time cooking and eating in Italy inspired us to develop many inventive pasta dishes based on Jamaican ingredients. In fact, these wicked island-style pasta dishes have become our signature, and we've had loads of fun creating and serving them. We share our all-time favorites with you here.

PENNE WITH ACKEE AND COCONUT CREAM SAUCE

This pasta was a favorite dish throughout our years in catering. It was a hit at every event, and always created quite a stir when our guests realized that ackee could be used in such an original and unexpected way. The combination of ackee paired with thyme, Scotch bonnet, and Parmesan cheese in a coconut cream sauce is delectable in a subtly exotic way.

Serves 6

2 tablespoons olive oil
1 medium yellow onion, chopped
1 stalk scallion, chopped
3 cloves garlic, minced
½ teaspoon seeded and minced Scotch bonnet
2 tablespoons chopped fresh thyme leaves, plus 6 sprigs for garnish
2 tablespoons chopped bell pepper
2 small plum tomatoes, peeled, seeded and diced
2 cups canned ackee, drained
sea salt and freshly ground black pepper
½ cup canned coconut milk
1½ cups heavy cream
1 (16-ounce) package penne pasta
⅔ cup freshly grated Parmesan cheese

Method

1 Heat the oil in saucepan over medium heat. Add the onion and cook for about 5 minutes until softened. Add the scallion, garlic, Scotch bonnet, thyme and bell pepper and cook, stirring occasionally, until the pepper is soft. Add the tomatoes, and when they begin to look cooked, fold in the ackee. Season with salt and pepper and cook for 2 to 3 minutes, until the ackee is well seasoned and all the flavors combined—don't stir too much! Add the coconut milk and bring to a boil. Add the heavy cream and bring to a boil again, then reduce the heat to a simmer and cook until slightly thickened. Season again with salt and pepper, and remove from the heat.

2 Cook the pasta in a large pot of salted boiling water until al dente, according to the package directions. Drain and return to the pot over medium heat; add the sauce and half of the Parmesan, toss to combine and taste and adjust the seasoning as necessary.

3 Transfer the pasta to individual serving bowls. Garnish each serving with a sprig of thyme and sprinkling with the remaining Parmesan.

JERKED CHICKEN LASAGNA

This white lasagna, made with béchamel sauce, caramelized onions, and bacon, and intensified by the spicy zip of jerked chicken breast, is sure to please almost any palate. And while there are many elements to this dish, once they are all prepared this is quick to put together.

Serves 10 to 12

6 (6- to 8-ounce) boneless skinless chicken breasts, cut into strips

3 tablespoons jerk seasoning, preferably Walker's Wood

3 tablespoons olive oil

8 cloves garlic, thinly sliced

6 medium yellow onions, sliced

sea salt and freshly ground pepper

1 (16-ounce) package bacon, chopped

1 (16-ounce) package lasagna noodles

1 tablespoon butter

¼ cup white wine

1 cup heavy cream

1 cup freshly grated Parmesan cheese

1 cup freshly shredded mozzarella cheese

For the Béchamel Sauce

2 tablespoons salted butter

1 teaspoon minced scallion

1 teaspoon minced garlic

2 teaspoons fresh thyme leaves

2 teaspoons all-purpose flour

1 cup whole milk

1 cup heavy cream

sea salt and freshly ground black pepper

Method

1 In a baking dish or resealable plastic bag, combine the chicken breasts with the jerk seasoning, tossing to ensure that the chicken is thoroughly coated. Let sit while you prepare the rest of the ingredients.

2 To make the béchamel sauce, melt the butter in a saucepan over medium heat. Add the scallion, garlic and thyme and cook for about 1 minute. Stir in the flour and cook for about 2 minutes until the flour is no longer raw tasting. Gradually add the milk and heavy cream, a little bit at a time, whisking during each addition, so that the sauce thickens but does not become lumpy. When the sauce has thickened, after about 5 minutes, season with salt and pepper and set aside.

3 In a medium skillet over medium-high heat, warm 1 tablespoon of the oil. Add the garlic and the chicken breasts and sauté for 5 minutes, until the chicken is no longer pink; transfer to a plate and set aside.

4 In a clean skillet, add the remaining 2 tablespoons oil and warm over medium heat. Add the onions and a sprinkle of salt. Lower the heat and cook until the onions are caramelized, 15 to 20 minutes. Transfer to a plate and set aside. Add the bacon to the same pan and sauté until cooked, about 6 minutes; transfer to a paper towel–lined plate and set aside.

5 Preheat the oven to 350°F. Boil the lasagne noodles in a large pot of salted water according to the package directions.

6 Meanwhile, in a small pot over medium heat, melt the butter. Add the wine and reduce by half. Pour in the heavy cream and bring to a boil. Reduce the heat and simmer until thickened, about 10 minutes. Off the heat, stir in ¼ cup of the Parmesan and set aside.

7 To assemble, spread a little of the béchamel sauce in the bottom of a lasagna dish. Follow with a third of the noodles, half of the chicken strips, crumbled bacon and caramelized onions, and then top with a third of the remaining béchamel, Parmesan and mozzarella. Repeat the layers in the same order, ending with the final third of noodles. Spread the remaining béchamel sauce over the entire dish and sprinkle with the remaining cheeses. Pour the cream sauce into the pockets of the lasagna.

8 Bake for about 25 minutes or until the cheese is browned and the lasagna is bubbly. Remove from the oven and let sit for about 10 minutes before serving.

CALLALOO AND RICOTTA RAVIOLI WITH TWO SAUCES

We served this dish for a wedding at the lighthouse in Negril. It was a beautiful but somewhat nerve-racking affair. The venue was spectacular, but it had no facilities, and we were serving a plated meal for two hundred people seated at long family-style tables—egad! As if that weren't challenging enough, the bride's Italian father was the producer of his own brand of olive oil and he wanted homemade ravioli with red and white sauce at the meal so much that he sent us recipes for the sauces. The pressure was on! We did not use his recipes, but instead came up with this version of the dish that incorporated some island flavor. The bride and groom were very happy, as was Papa.

COOKING HINT

Both of these sauces can stand on their own as a savory complement to any type of pasta. They can be made ahead of time, as can the ravioli. Refrigerate each sauce in an airtight container for up to 5 days. Spread the uncooked ravioli on sheet pans and place in the freezer. Once frozen, transfer the ravioli to an airtight container with waxed paper between each layer and freeze for up to 1 month.

Makes 24 to 30 raviolis (8 to 10 servings)

1 pound all-purpose flour

sea salt

2 large eggs

¾ cup warm water

3 tablespoons olive oil

½ yellow onion, chopped

1 stalk scallion, chopped

3 cloves garlic, minced

¼ teaspoon minced Scotch bonnet

1 bunch callaloo (or spinach, kale, arugula or collard greens), finely sliced (see page 23)

sea salt and freshly ground black pepper

½ teaspoon freshly grated nutmeg

½ pound ricotta cheese

1 egg whisked with 1 tablespoon water

freshly grated Parmesan cheese, torn fresh basil leaves and extra-virgin olive oil, for garnish

For the Scotchie Arrabiata Sauce

2 tablespoons olive oil, plus more for drizzling

4 cloves garlic, chopped

1 Scotch bonnet, seeded and chopped

1 yellow onion, chopped

1 bunch fresh thyme, chopped

12 plum tomatoes, peeled, seeded and diced

1 (14-ounce) can good-quality whole tomatoes, chopped

sea salt and freshly ground black pepper

For the Garlic and Thyme Cream Sauce

1 whole head garlic

1 tablespoon olive oil

2 tablespoons butter

½ stalk scallion, finely chopped

½ small onion, finely chopped

1 bunch fresh thyme, chopped

½ cup white wine

2½ cups heavy cream

Method

1 Sift the flour and ½ teaspoon salt into a large stainless-steel bowl. Make a crater in the center and pour in the eggs and warm water. Using a fork, partially incorporate the flour into the liquid, then knead the dough until well combined, 4 to 5 minutes. Wrap in plastic and chill in the refrigerator.

2 Warm 2 tablespoons oil in a large sauté pan over medium heat. Sweat the onion, scallion, garlic and Scotch bonnet for 3 to 5 minutes. Add the callaloo and cook down for about 5 minutes, then season with salt and pepper and a dash of nutmeg. Transfer to a fine-mesh sieve and squeeze out any excess liquid. Transfer to a bowl and stir in the ricotta; taste and adjust for salt if necessary.

3 Remove the dough from the refrigerator and lightly dust a sheet pan with flour. On a floured surface, roll out the dough ⅛ inch thick. Working in batches, cut out approximately eight 3-inch rounds. Place 1 teaspoon of the filling in the center of 4 rounds. Brush another 4 rounds of dough with the egg wash and place on top of the fillled rounds; press the edges of each ravioli together with the tines of a fork to seal. Set aside in a single layer on the prepared sheet pan; if you stack the ravioli, they will stick together. Continue with the rounds, filling, and egg wash until you've used up all the dough. Wrap the sheet pan with plastic and freeze until ready to cook.

4 To make the Scotchie arrabiata sauce, warm the oil in a medium saucepan over medium heat. Add the garlic, Scotch bonnet, onion and thyme and sauté for 5 minutes. Add the fresh plum tomatoes and their juices and cook for about 8 minutes. Stir in the canned tomatoes and their juice and bring to a boil. Reduce the heat to low and simmer for 20 minutes. Season with salt and pepper, remove from the heat and, using a blender, puree the sauce until smooth. Return the sauce to the pan over low heat, add a drizzle of oil and adjust the seasoning. Keep warm.

5 To make the garlic and thyme cream sauce, preheat the oven to 400°F. Chop the root end off the garlic, drizzle the whole head with the oil, wrap in foil, and roast for 30 minutes until tender when pierced with a knife. Meanwhile, melt the butter in a medium saucepan over medium heat, making sure it doesn't brown. Add the scallion, onion and thyme and cook for 5 to 10 minutes until softened. Add the white wine and reduce by half. Add the heavy cream and bring to a boil, then reduce the heat and simmer for 15 to 20 minutes, until the sauce thickens. Remove the roasted garlic from the oven, squeeze the cloves out of their skins onto a cutting board and smash with the back of a spoon. Whisk into the sauce and simmer for 5 minutes. Keep warm.

6 When you are ready to cook the ravioli, bring a large pot of water to a rolling boil and add the remaining 1 tablespoon oil and 1 teaspoon salt. Add the ravioli and cook for 10 to 15 minutes, until they float to the top. Using a slotted spoon, transfer to a colander to drain well.

7 Into the bottom of 8 warm pasta bowls, ladle the cream sauce to cover half of each bowl and the tomato sauce to cover the other half; the sauces should meet in the middle. Place three ravioli in each bowl on top of the sauces, garnish with Parmesan, fresh basil and a drizzle of extra-virgin olive oil and serve.

PRIMAVERA JAMAICANA

This dish, which is our take on a traditional Italian primavera, was a hugely popular item back in the day at Café Bella—so much so that years later, when I was developing a menu for Usain Bolt's Tracks and Records, we rebirthed and revamped a version of it as Ital Penne with Pumpkin Rundown. At Café Bella, we used spinach fettuccini; feel free to use any pasta you like.

Serves 6

1 tablespoon olive oil
1 tablespoon butter
1 bunch scallions, sliced
2 cloves garlic, chopped
1 inch fresh ginger, peeled and finely chopped
¼ Scotch bonnet, seeded and minced
2 tablespoons chopped fresh thyme
½ red pepper, sliced
½ very ripe plantain, peeled and cut into cubes
1 cup peeled calabaza pumpkin, cut into matchsticks
1 cho cho (chayote), peeled and cut into matchsticks (about 1 cup)
½ cup French beans (local string beans), trimmed
¼ cup Jamaican brandy or sherry
1½ cups heavy cream
1½ (14-ounce) cans coconut milk
¼ to ½ cup freshly grated Parmesan cheese, to taste
1 pound spinach fettuccine pasta
sea salt and freshly ground black pepper

Method

1 Warm the oil and butter in a large sauté pan over medium heat. When the butter is melted, add the scallions, garlic, ginger, Scotch bonnet, thyme and red pepper. Add the plantain and sauté for about 3 minutes. Add the pumpkin, cho cho and French beans. Add the brandy and cook until evaporated, about 5 minutes. Add the heavy cream and reduce for 1 to 2 minutes, then add the coconut milk and cook until thickened. Stir in the Parmesan and set aside.

2 Cook the pasta in boiling salted water until al dente according to the package directions. Drain and toss immediately with the vegetable mixture in the saucepan. Season again with salt and pepper and serve immediately.

COOKING HINT

For extra kick-ass flavor, add ½ cup chopped bacon in step 1, along with the onions and peppers, and cook until crispy.

If you are not serving this pasta (or any of our other pasta dishes) immediately, but want to be as ready as possible in advance, you can blanch the pasta then transfer it to an ice-water bath to shock it; this stops the cooking process. Toss the pasta with a little vegetable oil and hold covered until ready to use. Make sure to slightly undercook the pasta, because when you add it back to the pan with the sauce, it will continue to cook!

DOLCE JAMAICA

While we tend to prefer pasta with tomato sauce or simply tossed with some olive oil, it's just a fact that Jamaicans love creamy pasta sauces. This one is so yummy, with a hint of ginger and lots of fresh herbs, it's our go-to choice for last-minute entertaining or a simple dinner at home. It is easy, quick, appetizing and always a hit.

Serves 4 to 6

juice of 2 limes
2 teaspoons peeled, grated fresh ginger
1 clove garlic, chopped
¼ Scotch bonnet, seeded and diced
2 tablespoons fresh thyme leaves
2 tablespoons chopped fresh mint
2 tablespoons chopped fresh cilantro
3 tablespoons olive oil
sea salt and freshly ground black pepper
3 boneless skinless chicken breasts, halved
1 (16-ounce) package penne pasta
⅓ cup freshly grated Parmesan, for garnish

For the Cream Sauce

2 tablespoons butter
4 cloves garlic, minced
1 small yellow onion, finely diced
1 stalk scallion, thinly sliced
¼ Scotch bonnet, seeded and finely diced
2 tablespoons fresh thyme, chopped, plus
4 to 6 fresh sprigs, for garnish
¼ portobello mushroom, chopped
sea salt and freshly ground black pepper
½ cup sliced sun-dried tomatoes
½ cup white wine
1½ cups heavy cream
⅓ cup freshly grated Parmesan cheese

Method

1 In a baking dish or resealable plastic bag, combine the lime juice, ginger, garlic, Scotch bonnet, thyme, mint, cilantro, 1 tablespoon of the oil and salt and pepper. Add the chicken and marinate in the refrigerator for at least 1 hour.

2 To make the cream sauce, warm the butter in a medium saucepan over medium heat. Add the garlic, onion, scallion and Scotch bonnet and sauté until the onion is translucent, 3 to 5 minutes. Add the thyme and mushroom with a dash of salt and cook until the mushroom is soft, about 5 minutes. Add the sundried tomatoes and white wine and simmer until the wine evaporates, about 2 minutes. Add the heavy cream, bring to a simmer, then reduce the heat to low and simmer for 5 to 10 minutes, until the sauce has thickened. Remove from the heat and stir in the Parmesan. Season with salt and pepper and keep warm.

3 Heat the remaining 2 tablespoons oil in a large sauté pan over medium-high heat. Sear the chicken breasts until brown on the outside and juicy on the inside–don't overcook! (Alternatively, grill the chicken.) Transfer the chicken to a cutting board and cut into strips.

4 Cook the pasta in boiling salted water according to the package directions until al dente; drain, then immediately return to the pot, stir in the cream sauce, and season with salt and pepper.

5 Divide the pasta and sauce among serving bowls. Top each serving with sliced chicken, a sprig of thyme and Parmesan and serve immediately.

ROASTED TOMATO, EGGPLANT AND CHILE PASTA SALAD

Eggplants are called melangen in Trinidad and Tobago, and garden egg in Jamaica, where they grow easily but are not widely consumed as many people don't understand how to prepare them. This quick and easy dish is delectable—and requires almost no cleanup! It's a vegetarian option that everyone will love (for vegans, simply leave out the cheese), whether you're entertaining, eating a simple meal at home or need a dish to bring to an event.

Serves 6

2 small eggplants (about 1 pound total), sliced

8 plum tomatoes, quartered

2 onions, thickly sliced

8 cloves garlic, sliced

¾ cup olive oil (plus more if needed)

1 bunch fresh thyme, chopped

1 bunch fresh cilantro, chopped (plus more if needed)

½ Scotch bonnet, seeded and sliced into thin slivers

sea salt and freshly ground black pepper

1 pound pasta of your choice

4 ounces feta cheese, crumbled (optional)

Method

1 Preheat the oven to 375°F.

2 In a large bowl, toss the eggplants, tomatoes, onions and garlic with the oil, thyme, cilantro, and Scotch bonnet. Season with salt and pepper and transfer to a baking sheet, spread out in a single layer. Roast the vegetables for about 30 minutes, until the eggplant is moist and cooked through and the onions are caramelized.

3 Meanwhile, cook the pasta in boiling salted water according to the package directions; drain and let cool.

4 Roughly chop the roasted vegetables; toss with the pasta in a large bowl. Add more cilantro and oil, if necessary, then add the feta, if using, and toss to combine. Season with salt and pepper and serve at room temperature.

GINGER THYME RISOTTO

We blended Jamaican ginger with fresh thyme in this creamy risotto. It's scrumptious served as a side dish or on its own. Years ago, we paired it with fresh local marlin in a sherry glaze with grilled asparagus and crispy fried leeks alongside. But here we're giving it to you solo . . . so you can eat it alongside whatever you want.

Serves 10

6 tablespoons butter
¼ cup chopped yellow onion
3 tablespoons peeled, minced fresh ginger
2 tablespoons minced garlic
2 cups Arborio rice
½ cup dry white wine
1 cup sherry
1 quart hot chicken stock
3 tablespoons chopped fresh thyme (plus more as needed)
1¼ cups heavy cream
½ cup freshly grated Parmesan cheese
sea salt and freshly ground black pepper

Method

1 Melt the butter in a heavy-bottomed pan over medium heat. Add the onion, ginger and garlic and sweat for 1 to 2 minutes. Add the rice and cook, stirring frequently, until the tips of the rice appear white and all the grains are coated with oil. Add the white wine and ⅓ cup of the sherry and cook, stirring frequently, until the liquid is almost evaporated.

2 Add about one-third of the stock to the pan, stirring until the liquid has been absorbed into the rice. Add the remaining stock in two more additions, stirring constantly, until the liquid is absorbed and the rice begins to develop a creamy texture.

3 Add the remaining ⅔ cup sherry in the same manner, stirring constantly, and continue to cook until the rice is al dente and most of the liquid is absorbed; this should take 45 to 50 minutes in all.

4 Add the thyme, heavy cream and Parmesan and stir until the risotto thickens again. Season with salt and pepper, adjust the thyme, if necessary, and serve.

PASTA SALAD CUBANA À LA SUGARDADDIES

When we developed this menu item for a local Jamaican franchise, Sugardaddies, back in the year 2000, it was a novel dish indeed: penne with ripe plantain, lime vinaigrette, feta, black beans and corn. Ripe plantain is often featured in our dishes, in everything from salads to sandwiches to pastas and roasts. Sugardaddies is no longer around, but, boy, we still get requests for this pasta recipe, so here it is! This is a vegetarian entrée, but you can add grilled chicken breast to create a hearty pasta salad.

Serves 8 to 10

1 (16-ounce) package penne pasta
2 tablespoons vegetable oil
1 small ripe plantain, cut into cubes (about ¾ cup)
1 cup canned black beans
½ cup corn
½ red pepper, chopped (about ¼ cup)
½ red onion, chopped (about ¼ cup)
1 stalk scallion, thinly sliced
½ cup fresh cilantro leaves, chopped
1 cup crumbled feta cheese
sea salt and freshly ground black pepper

For the Lime Vinaigrette

2 tablespoons fresh lime juice
2 tablespoons olive oil
1 teaspoon ground cumin
2 tablespoons chopped fresh cilantro leaves
1 teaspoon minced garlic
sea salt and freshly ground pepper

Method

1 Cook the pasta in boiling salted water according to the package directions; drain and let cool.

2 Meanwhile, make the vinaigrette: In a small bowl, whisk together the lime juice, olive oil, cumin, cilantro and garlic until well combined. Season with salt and pepper.

3 In a small sauté pan, warm the vegetable oil over medium heat. Add the plantain and sauté for 5 to 10 minutes, until golden. Let cool.

4 In a large salad bowl, combine the pasta, black beans, corn, plaintain, red pepper, red onion, scallion, cilantro and feta. Add the vinaigrette and toss to combine. Season with salt and pepper. Let sit for at least 15 minutes to allow the flavors to meld.

5 Toss the salad once again and serve at room temperature.

THE WICKEDEST RIGATONI ALLA VODKA

This has always been one of our absolutely favorite pastas; anywhere we go, if it's on the menu we must order it to share! We both love pink sauce for its depth of flavor. We use jerk sausage from a local smokehouse, but you can subsitute any type of spicy sausage like chorizo. We add a dash of coconut milk for a hint of sweetness. If you want to add additional island flavor, substitute the Scotchie Arrabiata on page 67 for the basic tomato sauce (you'll need about 2 cups) but only if using the bacon.

Serves 4 to 6

For the Basic Tomato Sauce
2 tablespoons extra-virgin olive oil
1 medium onion, finely chopped
1 garlic clove, crushed
2 (14-ounce) cans whole tomatoes, chopped
½ cup white wine
1 bunch fresh basil, chopped
1 teaspoon chopped fresh thyme
sea salt and freshly ground black pepper

For the Vodka Sauce
3 tablespoons olive oil
½ yellow onion, chopped
4 ounces bacon or spicy sausage, diced
3 cloves garlic, minced
2 tablespoons chopped fresh thyme
¼ cup vodka
¼ cup coconut milk (optional)
½ to ¾ cup heavy cream, depending on whether you use coconut milk
sea salt and freshly ground black pepper

1 (16-ounce) package rigatoni pasta
⅔ cup freshly grated Parmesan cheese
3 tablespoons chopped fresh parsley

Method

1 To make the basic tomato sauce, warm the oil in a large saucepan over medium heat. Add the onion and garlic and sweat for about 5 minutes. Add the tomatoes and their juice and bring to a simmer over medium heat. Add the white wine, basil and thyme and return to a simmer. Reduce the heat to low and simmer gently, stirring occasionally, for about 30 minutes, until the sauce is thickened. If the sauce becomes too dry and starts to stick to the sides of the pan, add a few tablespoons of water. Season with salt and pepper and remove from the heat. Puree with a hand blender or in a food processor and set aside.

2 To make the vodka sauce, warm the oil in a large skillet over medium heat. Add the onion and cook for 5 minutes. Add the bacon or sausage and cook for another 5 minutes, then add the garlic and thyme. Cook until the bacon and sausage are cooked through, about 6 minutes.

3 Add the vodka and reduce until there is about 1 tablespoon left. Add the tomato sauce and bring to a simmer. Add the coconut milk, if using, and heavy cream and cook until thickened. Season with salt and pepper.

4 Meanwhile, cook the pasta in boiling salted water according to the package directions. Drain and return to the pot. Add the vodka sauce and half the Parmesan and toss well.

5 Taste and adjust the salt and pepper as necessary. Mix in the parsley and serve topped with the remaining Parmesan.

5

SUNDAY SUPPERS

ROASTS, STEWS AND FIXINGS

Sundays in the Caribbean are about family. All across the islands, families either dress up in their Sunday best and head to church for a few hours of fervent worship, or head off to the beach for a leisurely day of chilling in the sun. Either way, these activities build up quite an appetite, so they are typically followed by a hearty lunch.

We have many a fond childhood memory of Sunday meals, which always consisted of a tasty roast (pork with crackling, beef, chicken, or leg of lamb) served with roasted potatoes, rice and peas, fried ripe plantain, avocado, salad, macaroni pie and gravy. This was usually followed by a trip to the local ice cream parlor for a Sunday "cream." The lines were long, the wait eternal, but my-oh-my was it ever worth it!

In this chapter, we journey down memory lane and bring you some updated versions of our favorite Sunday lunches.

ROAST CHICKEN WITH CORNBREAD STUFFING

Every Caribbean island has its own version of roast chicken, and this is ours. We like to serve it with cornbread stuffing, as a change of pace from the white bread stuffing that is traditional. Serve with Rice and Peas (page 142), Rum and Brown Sugar Plantains (page 128) and Twice-Roasted Local Mixed Vegetables (page 132).

Serves 6

5 cloves garlic, minced
1 inch fresh ginger, peeled and grated
1 bunch fresh thyme, chopped
2 tablespoons soy sauce
1 tablespoon ground allspice
1 bunch scallion, sliced
½ teaspoon ground cinnamon
1 teaspoon minced Scotch bonnet
2 tablespoons olive oil
1 tablespoon brown sugar
sea salt and freshly ground black pepper
1 (5-pound) roasting chicken

For the Cornbread Stuffing

1 box cornbread or corn muffin mix
1 tablespoon butter
2 tablespoons olive oil
1 (16-ounce) package bacon, chopped
½ cup chopped yellow onion plus
1 small onion, sliced
½ cup chopped celery
¼ cup peeled and chopped carrot
2 cloves garlic, chopped, plus 2 whole cloves
1 bunch fresh thyme, chopped, plus 1 sprig
½ cup raisins
sea salt and freshly ground black pepper
2 plum tomatoes, chopped
1 whole Scotch bonnet
sprig of fresh rosemary
3 to 4 tablespoons white wine to taste
1 teaspoon brown sugar

Method

1 In a small bowl, combine the garlic, ginger, thyme, soy sauce, allspice, scallions, cinnamon, Scotch bonnet, oil, brown sugar and salt and pepper; mix to form a paste. Rub the paste all over the chicken and inside the cavity. Let sit in the refrigerator for at least 1 hour (preferably overnight).

2 To make the stuffing, bake the cornbread in a sheet pan according to the package directions. Let cool, then cut into 1-inch cubes.

3 Preheat the oven to 400°F.

4 In a large saucepan, melt the butter with the oil over medium heat; pour half of the melted butter and oil mixture into a small bowl and reserve. In the butter and oil remaining in the pan, sauté the bacon for about 5 minutes until it begins to brown. Add the chopped onion, celery and carrot and cook for another 5 minutes, stirring occasionally. Add the chopped garlic, chopped thyme and raisins and cook for about 3 minutes. Add the cornbread cubes, stir to coat and season with salt and pepper. Remove from the heat.

5 Place half of the stuffing in a serving dish; don't allow this stuffing to touch the raw chicken, as it will just be warmed for serving. Stuff the remaining half of the stuffing into the cavity of the chicken and place the chicken in a roasting pan, on a rack if desired. Pour the reserved butter and olive oil mixture over the chicken and roast for 15 minutes, then reduce the heat to 350°F and roast for another 30 to 35 minutes, until the juices run clear when a knife tip is inserted into a leg joint (165°F on an instant-read thermometer). Transfer the chicken to a cutting board.

6 Transfer the pan juices to a saucepan. Add the tomatoes, sliced onion, garlic cloves, Scotch bonnet, thyme and rosemary sprigs and simmer over medium-low heat until the vegetables are softened, about 10 minutes. Stir in the white wine and brown sugar and add water if necessary. Transfer the gravy to a serving bowl.

7 Remove the stuffing from the chicken and mound it in the center of a platter. Carve the chicken and place alongside the stuffing. Serve with the extra stuffing and gravy on the side.

RIB ROAST WITH MUSHROOM GRAVY

Many summer holidays were spent in London with our aunt Winsome, who judged every event to be a success or failure by the quality and quantity of the food. She was known for her enormous appetite even though she was not overweight. Her daughter Caroline was our constant companion from as young as three years old to our early twenties, as our families vacationed together. We shared many a meal of roast beef and Yorkshire pudding that was, and still continues to be, a family favorite.

Serves 8 to 10

2 tablespoons soy sauce or Worcestershire sauce
4 tablespoons olive oil
1 bunch fresh rosemary, chopped
2 bunches fresh thyme, chopped
6 cloves garlic, minced
1 yellow onion, finely chopped, plus 2 yellow onions quartered
½ Scotch bonnet, seeded and minced
sea salt and freshly ground black pepper
1 (7- to 8-pound) boneless rib roast
6 small roasting potatoes, halved or quartered depending on size
8 large carrots, peeled and chopped
4 cho cho (chayote), peeled and chopped

For the Mushroom Gravy
¼ cup red wine
pat of butter
6 ounces button mushrooms
handful of shiitake mushroom caps
1 small yellow onion, chopped
3 plum tomatoes, chopped
3 whole cloves garlic
1 cup beef stock
½ teaspoon sugar
1 bay leaf
cornstarch (optional)

Method

1 In a small bowl, combine the soy sauce, 2 tablespoons oil, rosemary, 1 bunch of the thyme, garlic, chopped onion, Scotch bonnet and salt and pepper to form a paste that is slightly wet. With a sharp knife, score holes in the beef and generously stuff the paste deep into the holes. Rub the remaining paste all over the exterior of the beef, followed by a generous rubbing with sea salt. Place the roast in a baking dish, cover with plastic and refrigerate for at least 12 hours. Let come to room temperature before cooking (about 1 hour).

2 Preheat the oven to 375°F.

3 Transfer the beef onto a rack in a roasting pan and roast for about 30 minutes.

4 Meanwhile, in a large bowl, toss the potatoes, carrots, quartered onions and cho cho with the remaining 2 tablespoons oil and the remaining bunch of thyme; season with salt. After the beef has cooked for about 30 minutes, add the vegetables to the base of the roasting pan so that the drippings from the beef will baste the vegetables during cooking. Cook for another 40 to 45 minutes, until the potatoes are fork-tender. Transfer the potatoes and other vegetables to a plate and test the meat with an instant-read thermometer inserted in the thickest part. If it reads 140° to 145°F, you'll have a medium doneness. Transfer the meat to a cutting board.

5 To make the mushroom gravy, place the roasting pan with the drippings on the stovetop. Skim off any excess fat, then add the red wine and deglaze the pan. Add a dab of butter along with the mushrooms, onion, tomatoes and garlic cloves and cook for about 5 minutes. Add the beef stock, sugar and bay leaf and simmer for another 10 minutes until it thickens slightly. Thicken with a little cornstarch, if necessary.

6 Carve the beef and serve with the roasted vegetables and mushroom gravy on the side.

MUMMY'S ROAST PORK WITH CRACKLIN' AND RUM GRAVY

Our mother is a master at making roast pork with cracklin'. The cracklin' is always absolutely perfect, and though we know all too well that it might not be good for the heart, there is literally a fight for the cracklin' when it comes out of the oven. Mummy now hides it until it's time to eat. Between Liam, Jude (a self-declared carnivore) and our father, the likelihood of the ladies even getting one bite of the cracklin' is slim to none—which is why it's always good to know where the hiding spot is so we can "teif" a little! Here is Mummy's technique for outrageously good cracklin', every single time.

Serves 8 to 10

1 inch fresh ginger, peeled and roughly chopped

4 cloves garlic, roughly chopped, plus 8 whole cloves

2 bunches fresh thyme, roughly chopped

2 stalks scallions, roughly chopped

¼ small yellow onion, roughly chopped, plus 1 large yellow onion, quartered

½ Scotch bonnet, seeded and chopped, plus 1 whole

sea salt

1 tablespoon olive oil

2 tablespoons soy sauce

1 (8-pound) pork leg with a good skin and fat

4 to 6 limes

6 to 8 potatoes, quartered, with skin on

1 tablespoon chopped fresh rosemary

freshly ground black pepper

2 bay leaves

3 tablespoons rum

3 plum tomatoes, chopped

Method

1 In a food processor or blender, combine the ginger, chopped garlic, half of the thyme, the scallions, the chopped onion, the chopped Scotch bonnet, 2 teaspoons salt, the oil and 1 tablespoon of the soy sauce and blend to form a paste. Using a sharp knife, score holes all over the pork leg and stuff the paste into the holes. Rub the remaining paste to coat the outside of the meat. Place the pork leg, skin side up, in a roasting pan and pat the fat dry—be sure not to place it skin side down, where it may soak in liquid, or you won't achieve successful cracklin'. Refrigerate, uncovered, for at least 4 hours, to allow the skin to dry out.

2 Preheat the oven to 500°F. Remove the chilled pork from the fridge, pat the skin dry again and score lines in the skin in a criss-cross pattern. Squeeze the limes onto the skin, then rub the roast generously with a little less than 1 tablespoon salt. Repeat this process five times: squeezing lime juice onto the skin, then rubbing it with salt. Place the pork on a rack in a roasting pan, then place the cold meat in a piping hot oven (the heat will draw the fat out of the skin and make the cracklin' good and crispy). Roast the pork for about 40 minutes. Do not turn the pork or baste it; it must stay skin side up.

3 Meanwhile, in a large bowl, toss the potatoes with the rosemary, quartered onion and salt and pepper to taste, and set aside.

4 The cracklin' will finish cooking before the pork. After about 30 minutes, you will see the skin of the pork beginning to bubble. After 40 to 45 minutes, when the skin is bubbly, brown, and crispy around the edges, the cracklin' is done. Remove the meat from the oven and cut away the skin from the leg, leaving some fat on top of the leg. (It should come off easily, as the skin will have separated from the fat by now.)

5 Reduce the oven temperature to 400°F. Pour out all the fat drippings from the bottom of the roasting pan into a measuring cup and skim off the excess fat. Take 2 tablespoons of this pork fat and toss with the seasoned

potatoes and onion. Place the pork in the center of the pan without the rack with the potatoes and onions surrounding it. Pour the rest of the fat drippings over the pork and potatoes and return the pan to the oven. Cook the pork, turning and basting as necessary, for about 1½ hours more or until the meat is cooked through and an instant-read thermometer inserted into the thickest part of the leg registers at least 160°F. Transfer the meat to a cutting board and the vegetables to a plate and set aside.

6 If there is a lot of fat in the drippings, pour the cooking liquid into a glass jar or bowl and place in the fridge. Once it has cooled a little, skim the fat off the top of the drippings and place the drippings in a saucepan. Add the garlic cloves, remaining thyme, the bay leaves, the whole Scotch bonnet, the remaining 1 tablespoon soy sauce, the rum and tomatoes and simmer until the tomatoes are cooked, about 15 minutes.

7 Carve the pork and place it on a platter, mounding the potatoes and onions around the meat. Chop the cracklin' and arrange it around the edges of the platter as a garnish. Serve with the gravy on the side.

BAKED HAM WITH ORTANIQUE GINGER GLAZE

We always make this wonderful ham leading into the holiday season, and while our family doesn't serve ham at Christmas dinner, we keep this in the fridge for a quick meal and an even quicker sandwich. The ham bone makes an awesomely delicious gungo pea soup that's perfect for Boxing Day lunch. Extremely sweet, an ortanique is a cross between a Valencia orange and a tangerine; if you aren't lucky enough to find one, substitute another sweet orange instead.

Serves 12

1 (12- to 15-pound) ready-to-eat
bone-in ham
3 tablespoons ortanique or orange zest
3 cups fresh ortanique or orange juice
1 cup brown sugar, plus more for sprinkling
1 inch fresh ginger, peeled and grated
handful of allspice berries
½ cup Dijon mustard, plus more for serving
handful of whole cloves
1 ortanique, sliced
fruit chutney, for serving

Method

1 Preheat the oven to 350°F. Peel the skin off the ham and score the fat in a diamond shape.

2 In a small saucepan, simmer the ortanique zest and juice, brown sugar, ginger and allspice over medium heat, until the sugar is melted and the glaze is slightly thickened, about 15 minutes.

3 Set the ham in a baking dish, spread the top with the mustard and sprinkle with some brown sugar. Insert the cloves in the top of the ham. Pour half of the glaze over the ham.

4 Bake the ham for 1½ hours, basting frequently with the glaze. In the last 30 minutes, add the ortanique slices to the top of the ham in a decorative pattern, securing them with toothpicks. Bake and baste until the top of the ham is caramelized and sticky.

5 Transfer the juices from the bottom of the pan to a sauce bowl. Carve the ham and garnish with orantique slices. Place the ham on a platter and serve with Dijon mustard, fruit chutney and the pan juices on the side.

SUZIE'S SUNDAY ROAST PORK CHOPS

So here's the thing: I love turning up unannounced at my sister's house on a Sunday because there is always the most delightful spread and I get to (selfishly) indulge without doing any of the work. Suzie's pork chops are infamous—they're simple and absolutely delicious with the combination of Asian flavors and surprise burst of mint. All I have to do is arrive and settle in like one of the kids, extending my plate for seconds when the time comes.—MICHELLE

Serves 4 to 6

1 teaspoon orange zest
¼ cup orange juice
2 tablespoons peeled, grated fresh ginger
2 tablespoons soy sauce
1 bunch fresh cilantro, chopped
1 bunch fresh thyme, chopped
3 tablespoons hoisin sauce
3 tablespoons barbeque sauce (optional)
2 tablespoons honey
2 small yellow onions, roughly chopped, plus 1 small yellow onion, sliced
6 cloves garlic, chopped
8 pork chops (about 6 ounces each)
2 plum tomatoes, chopped
¼ bell pepper, sliced
1 tablespoon chopped fresh mint
1 cup water

Method

1 In a small bowl, combine the orange zest and juice, ginger, soy sauce, cilantro, thyme, 2 tablespoons of the hoisin sauce, and barbeque sauce, if using, 1 tablespoon of the honey, the chopped onions, and garlic. Place the pork chops in a baking dish and pour the marinade over the chops, making sure it covers them well. Let marinate in the refrigerator for at least 4 hours in the fridge.

2 Preheat the oven to 400°F.

3 Transfer the chops and marinade to a flameproof roasting pan, arrange the chops in a single layer, and roast for 40 to 50 minutes, turning the chops over halfway through, until the pork is cooked through and soft.

4 Transfer the pan with the pork chops and marinade (now enriched with pan drippings) to the stovetop over medium heat. Add the tomatoes, sliced onion, bell pepper, mint and water over and around the chops and mix into the marinade. Stir in the remaining 1 tablespoon each of honey and hoisin sauce and bring to a boil; reduce the heat to low, cover the pan with aluminium foil and simmer for 20 minutes. The chops will be juicy, soft and tasty after cooking in their own liquid. Serve hot.

MARMALADE-GLAZED LEG OF LAMB

Leg of lamb is a favorite of ours and brings back many childhood memories of our summers in England with Aunt Winsome. Many Sundays were spent lunching in the English countryside on lamb, roast potatoes, mint sauce and stolen sips of Pimms! Instead of the traditional leg of lamb with mint sauce or jelly, we add a touch of fresh ginger and Scotch bonnet to the marinade and baste the lamb with a marmalade glaze. Feel free to serve a jelly of some sort on the side as well, or just drizzle a little of the marmalade glaze over the carved meat. Delish!

Serves 6 to 8

2 cloves garlic, minced
½ Scotch bonnet, minced
1 tablespoon grated orange zest
2 teaspoons fresh chopped sage
1 tablespoon chopped fresh thyme
2 teaspoons peeled, grated fresh ginger
2 tablespoons soy sauce
¼ cup extra-virgin olive oil
2 tablespoons Appleton Estate V/X rum (or any dark rum)
sea salt and freshly ground pepper
1 (4-pound) boneless leg of lamb

For the Rum and Marmalade Glaze

(MAKES ABOUT ¾ CUP)
½ cup orange marmalade
½ cup orange juice
2 teaspoons brown sugar
2 tablespoons chopped fresh thyme
¼ cup Appleton Estate V/X Rum (or any dark rum)

Method

1 In a medium bowl, combine the garlic, Scotch bonnet, orange zest, sage, thyme, ginger, soy sauce, oil and rum. Whisk until blended; season with salt and pepper. Place the leg of lamb in a baking dish and pour the marinade over the lamb, working it into the meat with your hands. Refrigerate for a minimum of 3 hours.

2 Let the lamb come to room temperature before roasting. Preheat the oven to 350°F.

3 To make the rum and marmalade glaze, combine the marmalade, orange juice, brown sugar and thyme in a small saucepan. Simmer over medium heat until syrupy, 10 minutes. Whisk in the rum and simmer for 1 minute.

4 Roast the lamb for 1 to 1½ hours, depending on the size of the leg, repeatedly basting with the marmalade glaze. For medium doneness, an instant-read thermometer inserted into the thickest part of the leg should register 140° to 145°F. Let stand for 5 to 10 minutes before carving and serving.

HYACINTH'S POT ROAST

Hyacinth, who has worked with us for a very long time, has a stable of go-to recipes. This is one of our favorites. We like to serve this with rice and peas (page 142), fried ripe plantains and whatever seasonal root vegetables are on hand. The Cho Cho Packets (page 132) would also go very well with it.

Serves 6

3 tablespoons mixed herbs (such as mint, basil, thyme and rosemary), chopped
1 bunch scallions, chopped
1 yellow onion, finely chopped, plus 1 yellow onion, chopped
½ Scotch bonnet, seeded and finely chopped, plus 1 whole
2 teaspoons sea salt, plus more for seasoning
2 teaspoons freshly ground black pepper, plus more for seasoning
1 inch fresh ginger, peeled and grated
6 cloves garlic, minced, plus 8 whole
1 tablespoon olive oil
1 tablespoon soy sauce
5 pounds beef pot roast, trimmed
3 tablespoons vegetable oil
1 carrot, peeled and chopped
2 plum tomatoes, diced
1 bunch fresh thyme, chopped, plus more for seasoning
¼ cup white wine (optional)
1 teaspoon sugar
1 tablespoon water mixed with 1 teaspoon cornstarch for a slurry (optional)

Method

1 In a small bowl, mix together the herbs, scallions, finely chopped onion, chopped Scotch bonnet, salt, pepper, ginger, minced garlic, olive oil and soy sauce. Using a sharp knife, score small holes in the roast and stuff the marinade in the holes, then rub the remaining marinade all over the outside of the meat. If the roast is loose, tie it together with kitchen twine to make it easier to carve later. Place in a baking dish and let sit in the refrigerator for at least 2 hours.

2 Heat the vegetable oil in a large Dutch oven over medium-high heat. Wipe off any excess marinade from the meat and sear on all sides until browned. Add a touch of water, cover the pot and cook over low heat for about 30 minutes. Keep adding water a little at a time as the existing water evaporates. Don't add a lot of water at once; we want the meat to make its own flavorful gravy.

3 After 30 minutes, add the carrot, tomatoes, chopped onion, garlic cloves, thyme and whole Scotch bonnet to the pan. (Be careful not to burst the pepper, as we want the Scotch bonnet flavor without its interior heat.) Keep adding water, a little at a time, until the meat is cooked through, about 20 minutes.

4 Transfer the meat to a cutting board and let rest. Return the pot with the pan juices and vegetables to the stovetop over medium heat. Adjust the seasoning of the gravy with the white wine, if using, and more thyme, salt, pepper and sugar as needed. If you want to thicken the gravy, whisk in the cornstarch slurry.

5 Carve the roast, transfer to a platter and pour the gravy over the meat, reserving some gravy to serve on the side.

COUNTRY-STYLE SHEPHERD'S PIE

Shepherd's pie is the ultimate comfort food. "Mince," or cooked ground beef, reminds us of our grandmother, MaMa, as she would always cook it for us when we came home for school break. This updated version incorporates both sweet potato and white potato: a layer of mashed sweet potato at the base is covered with mince and then topped with a layer of regular mashed potatoes. It's a yummy one-pot meal that is sure to please.

Serves 6 to 8

4 tablespoons soy sauce, plus more
if necessary
2 bunches fresh thyme, chopped
4 cloves garlic, chopped, plus 3 cloves garlic,
finely chopped
½ Scotch bonnet, minced, plus ½ teaspoon
minced
2 teaspoons sea salt, plus more for seasoning
3 pounds ground beef
2 pounds white potatoes, peeled and cubed
2 pounds sweet potatoes, peeled and cubed
2 tablespoons salted butter, plus more
for greasing
½ cup grated Cheddar cheese
½ cup whole milk
freshly ground white pepper
1 tablespoon olive oil
1 yellow onion, finely chopped
1 carrot, peeled and diced
1 sweet pepper, diced
2 plum tomatoes, chopped
1 teaspoon tomato paste
¼ cup white wine
¼ cup grated Parmesan cheese

Method

1 In a large bowl, whisk together 2 tablespoons of the soy sauce, half of the thyme, the chopped garlic, the ½ minced Scotch bonnet and salt. Add the ground beef, toss to coat and set aside.

2 Meanwhile, put a large pot of salted water on to boil. First add the white potatoes and cook for 20 minutes. Using a slotted spoon, transfer to a plate. Add the sweet potatoes to the same pot and boil until cooked through, about 20 minutes.

3 While the sweet potatoes are boiling, mash the white potatoes with half the butter, half the Cheddar and half the milk. Season with salt and white pepper and set aside. Drain and transfer the sweet potato to a plate and mash with the remaining butter, Cheddar and milk. Season with salt and pepper again and set aside.

4 Preheat the oven to 375°F.

5 Heat the oil in a pan over medium heat. Add the onion, the finely chopped garlic, the ½ teaspoon Scotch bonnet, carrot, sweet pepper and remaining thyme and sauté for about 5 minutes, until softened. Add the marinated beef and sauté, breaking up the ground beef with a spatula, for 10 minutes. Stir in the remaining 2 tablespoons soy sauce, the tomatoes, tomato paste and white wine and cook until the tomatoes break down and much of the liquid has evaporated. Season with salt and pepper.

6 Brush the base of a casserole dish with butter and pack the mashed sweet potato in the bottom of the dish. Top with a layer of the beef mixture and cover with a layer of the mashed potatoes. Sprinkle with the Parmesan and bake for 20 minutes, or until golden brown. Cool for 10 minutes before serving.

ROAST SALMON WITH CITRUS GINGER AÏOLI

This is the easiest and quickest "Sunday roast" you will ever cook. Roast salmon makes for a much lighter version of your typical Sunday meal—and, hey, who says your roast has to be meat? Salmon is not indigenous to the Caribbean but works surprisingly well when infused with Caribbean flavors like ginger and citrus.

Serves 4 to 6

3 tablespoons olive oil
juice of 1 orange
juice of 1 lime
1 bunch fresh rosemary, chopped
1 inch ginger, peeled and grated
4 cloves garlic
sea salt and freshly ground black pepper
1 (2- to 2½-pound) side of salmon, skin on
2 oranges, thinly sliced

For the Citrus Ginger Aïoli

juice and zest of 1 orange
1 cup mayonnaise
1 teaspoon Dijon mustard
2 tablespoons olive oil
1 teaspoon minced garlic
1 teaspoon peeled and grated fresh ginger
sea salt and freshly ground black pepper

Method

1 Preheat the oven to 500°F.

2 In a small bowl, combine the oil, orange and lime juices, rosemary, ginger and garlic and season with salt and pepper. Place the salmon in a large baking dish and pour the marinade on top. Arrange the orange slices on top of the salmon. Let marinate in the refrigerator for about 1 hour.

3 To make the citrus ginger aïoli, in a small bowl, simply whisk together the orange juice and zest, mayonnaise, mustard, oil, garlic and ginger until well combined. Season with salt and pepper. Cover the bowl with plastic wrap and refrigerate.

4 Transfer the fish, skin side down, to a large, shallow roasting pan and roast for 15 minutes. Reduce the oven temperature to 425°F and roast until cooked through (the fish should be flaky but still moist), 5 to 10 minutes.

5 Transfer the whole side of salmon to a platter and serve hot or at room temperature, drizzled with some of the aïoli. Serve with the roasted orange slices and the remaining aïoli on the side.

6

OXTAIL, MY ASS!

THE CLASSICS, REVISTED

No Caribbean cookbook would be complete without recipes for some of the more traditional stews and one-pot dishes found throughout the region. In this chapter, we share our versions of some good old-fashioned home cooking, with our own special twists, like adding fresh mango, white rum and coconut milk to our curry goat.

The best cooks in the Caribbean are the home cooks, mostly women, who spend a good portion of their time creating and serving meals for their families. They make home that special place where the kitchen is filled with the aroma of tasty dishes like the ones in this chapter, which welcome friends and strangers alike, the minute they cross the threshold.

MUMMY'S "CHINESE" CHICKEN WITH ORANGE, GINGER AND RUM

Our mother makes this wonderful unique chicken dish; it's a really nice change from the typical stewed chicken or fricassee chicken that we make in so many of the islands. We love the Asian influences combined with the island rum and the citrus.

Serves 6

3 tablespoons soy sauce
2 inches fresh ginger, peeled and grated
6 cloves garlic, chopped
freshly ground black pepper
1 (4-pound) whole chicken, cut in half
¼ cup vegetable, peanut or sesame oil
¼ cup mushroom soy sauce
1 cup water
1 teaspoon orange zest, or more to taste
2 tablespoons brown sugar, or more to taste
2 tablespoons rum, or more to taste
5 star anise seeds
1 stalk scallion, sliced, for garnish
fresh cilantro, for garnish

Method

1 In a baking dish, combine the soy sauce, half of the ginger, half of the garlic and a generous grind of pepper. Add the chicken halves, toss well and let marinate in the refrigerator for at least 30 minutes.

2 Heat the oil in a medium pan over medium-high heat until very hot. Place the chicken halves in the pan, skin side down, and sear. Turn the chicken over to sear the other side. Mix the soy sauce with the water and pour it over the chicken. Add the remaining ginger and garlic and bring to a boil, then lower the heat and simmer for 20 minutes. Add the orange zest, brown sugar, rum and star anise and simmer for 8 to 10 more minutes, until the sauce is thickened and the chicken is cooked through.

3 Transfer the chicken to a cutting board and let cool, then chop into bite-size pieces. Adjust the seasoning of the sauce with more sugar, zest or rum as necessary, and reduce to thicken a bit more, about 5 minutes.

4 Divide the chicken among serving plates, pour the sauce over the chicken and garnish with the scallions and cilantro.

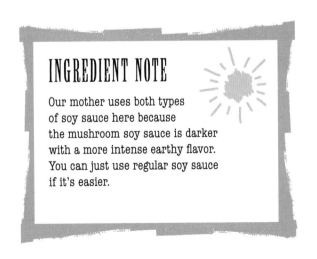

INGREDIENT NOTE

Our mother uses both types of soy sauce here because the mushroom soy sauce is darker with a more intense earthy flavor. You can just use regular soy sauce if it's easier.

OXTAIL WITH BROAD BEANS

If there is one item that we would consider "hungry belly" food, it would be oxtail, the singular favorite dish of many a Jamaican man far and wide. The oxtails are simmered down in a thick, rich gravy with broad beans, spinners (or flour dumplings) and vegetables and served over a mound of rice and peas. In this version, we use a technique we learned from a former employee, Daphne, that makes supremely tender oxtails and delicious gravy: Use ice rather than water to create the cooking liquid for the oxtail, adding more ice a little at a time as the water evaporatates. Alternatively, you can simply use water (adding a little at a time) or cook the oxtails in a pressure cooker, which shortens the cooking time.

Serves 6

1 yellow onion, chopped
3 stalks scallions, sliced, plus 1 bunch scallions, roughly chopped
8 cloves garlic, chopped
½ Scotch bonnet, seeded and chopped, plus 1 whole Scotch bonnet (optional)
½ cup water
3 pounds oxtails, trimmed
2 tablespoons soy sauce, plus more to taste
2 teaspoons sea salt, plus more for seasoning
1 teaspoon freshly ground black pepper, plus more for seasoning
1 bunch fresh thyme leaves, chopped, plus 1 bunch thyme sprigs
4 tablespoons vegetable oil
2 (15-ounce) cans broad beans, drained

For the Spinners

1½ cups all-purpose flour
pinch of sea salt
½ cup water

Method

1 In a medium bowl, combine half the onion, the 3 sliced scallions, half the garlic and the chopped Scotch bonnet with the water. In a baking dish, rub the oxtails with 1 tablespoon of the soy sauce, salt, pepper and chopped thyme. Pour the seasoning ingredients over the oxtails and marinate in the refrigerator for 24 hours to flavor and tenderize the meat.

2 Heat 2 tablespoons of the oil in a deep pot over high heat. Working in batches, place a single layer of oxtails in the pot and brown them, about 5 minutes per side. Transfer the browned meat to a plate and set aside. Add a little more oil only if necessary, as the fat rendered from the meat will give you additional oil, and repeat with the rest of the oxtails in batches, about 30 minutes total.

3 Add 1 cup water to the pan drippings and scrape up the browned bits from the bottom of the pan and pour into a bowl; set aside. Return the oxtails to the pot and add the remaining onion, chopped scallions, remaining garlic, thyme sprigs, the whole Scotch bonnet, if using, and the remaining 1 tablespoon soy sauce and sauté for about 5 minutes over high heat, making sure the oxtail is well coated. Cover the meat with a layer of ice, cover the pot, and simmer the meat.

4 After about 40 minutes, return the pan drippings to the pot and cook the oxtails slowly over medium to medium-high heat. Keep adding ice, a little at a time, making sure there is just enough liquid to cover the meat until the oxtails are tender and cooked through (you can also use water in lieu of ice), about 2 hours.

5 Meanwhile, make the spinners: Whisk together the flour and salt in a small bowl. Add the water and knead until the dough forms a mass. Shape the dough into a ball and let it rest for at least 15 minutes.

6 After the meat has been cooking for about 2 hours, take small pieces of dough, roll them into "cigarettes" and place them directly in the simmering liquid in the pot. Add the broad beans and simmer for another 30 minutes or so, until the liquid is thick. Taste and adjust the seasoning and serve.

CURRIED GOAT WITH WHITE RUM AND FRESH MANGO

Everyone in Jamaica loves "a curry goat." In fact, many festive occasions as well as funerals and wakes are commemorated with the slaughter of a goat as a blessing, as it is a widely held local superstition that the letting of blood wards away evil sprits and protects the living. The goat meat is cooked down in a Dutch oven or "dutchie" over an outdoor flame for many hours. The remaining parts of the goat are never wasted; they're used to make a hearty soup called Mannish Water. Even the goat's testicles are included, as they are supposed to give added virility and stamina to the males who drink it. (We think this is an acquired taste and can't pretend we are fans.) In our version, we modernize curry goat a bit by adding some fresh mango, white rum and coconut milk, and serve it up with a fresh banana raisin salsa, toasted grated coconut, toasted peanuts and cashews, rice and store-bought roti.

Serves 6 to 8

Banana Raisin Salsa
4 medium ripe bananas, diced
¼ cup raisins
2 tablespoons finely diced red onion
2 tablespoons chopped fresh cilantro
1 tablespoon fresh lime juice
1 tablespoon chopped fresh mint

1 large onion, finely chopped
7 stalks scallion, finely chopped
8 cloves garlic, finely chopped
1 inch ginger, peeled and finely chopped
1 Scotch bonnet, finely chopped
4 tablespoons curry powder
¾ cup plus 1 tablespoon vegetable oil
1 bunch fresh thyme
sea salt and freshly ground black pepper
3½ pounds boneless goat (or lamb) meat, cut into 1-inch pieces
about 4 cups water
1 (14-ounce) can coconut milk
¼ cup white rum
12 whole allspice berries
2 carrots (about 1 pound), peeled and diced
1 potato (about ½ pound), peeled and diced
½ cup diced fresh ripe mango

Method

1 To make the banana raisin salsa, combine all the ingredients and let sit for at least 2 hours until the flavors blend.

2 In a large bowl, combine the onion, scallions, garlic, ginger and Scotch bonnet. Transfer half the onion mixture to a baking dish and add 3 tablespoons of the curry powder, the 1 tablespoon oil, the thyme, 1 tablespoon salt and 1 teaspoon pepper. Add the goat meat, toss to coat the meat with the spice rub and marinate for at least 30 minutes.

3 Heat 2 tablespoons oil in a large pot over medium-high heat. Sear the goat in batches to not overcrowd the pan, then transfer to a bowl and set aside. Deglaze the pan with a little water to get all of the scrapings from the bottom of the pan, and then pour over the seared meat.

4 In the same pot, heat another 2 tablespoons oil and add the remaining 1 tablespoon curry powder to toast the curry for about 1 minute. Add the remaining onion mixture and cook for about 2 minutes, then stir in the seared goat meat and cooking liquid. Add about 4 cups water (or just enough to cover the goat meat) and bring to a boil. Cook over high heat for about 40 minutes.

5 Add the coconut milk, rum and allspice to the pot and cook for another 15 minutes, adding more liquid as needed. Add the carrots, potato and mango and cook for about 35 minutes more, until the goat meat is tender.

6 Divide the goat, vegetables and mango among individual bowls and pour over the sauce. Serve with the salsa, along with the array of condiments noted above.

TRINIDADIAN CHICKEN AND RICE (PELAU)

Pelau will always remind us of our time living in Trinidad. This one-pot dish of chicken, rice, pigeon peas, coconut milk and vegetables is so good that you will keep eating it for days after it is made. This recipe calls for the quintessential "green seasoning" that is the basis of all Trini cooking; this amazing seasoning blend can be used as a marinade for many meats and as a flavor enhancer for many dishes. This delicious recipe comes courtesy of our Trini friend Cree, who has saved our lives with her incredible pelau on many occasions during Trinidad Carnival, when we roll in exhausted from a night of debaucherous behavior—and one too many glasses of rum. Thanks, Cree.

Serves 12

For the Trini-Style Green Seasoning

4 stalks scallion, chopped
1 bunch fresh thyme
2 bunches fresh chadon beni (culantro)
or cilantro
1 bunch fresh parsley
12 cloves garlic, peeled
1 large yellow onion, peeled and
roughly chopped
1 Scotch bonnet (optional)
6 pimiento peppers
3 tablespoons distilled white vinegar
3 tablespoons vegetable oil
sea salt and freshly ground black pepper

1 tablespoon soy sauce
1 teaspoon ketchup
3 tablespoons vegetable oil
sea salt and freshly ground black pepper
1 (3-pound) chicken, cut into parts
2 cups dried pigeon peas, soaked overnight
3 tablespoons brown sugar
2 cups canned coconut milk
2 cups parboiled rice, washed and drained
¾ cup chopped onions
1 cup peeled and chopped calabaza pumpkin
½ cup peeled and chopped carrots
1 whole Scotch bonnet
½ cup sliced scallions

Method

1 To make the Trini-style green seasoning, puree the scallions, thyme, chadon beni, parsley, garlic, onion, Scotch bonnet, pimiento peppers, vinegar and oil in a blender. Remove to a baking dish and season with salt and pepper.

2 Add the soy sauce, ketchup and 1 tablespoon of the oil to the green seasoning. Season with salt and pepper, add the chicken and set aside while you cook the peas.

3 In a small pot, cover the peas with salted water and bring to a boil. Reduce the heat to medium-low and simmer for 30 to 35 minutes, until the peas are cooked. Drain the peas and reserve the cooking liquid.

4 Heat the remaining 2 tablespoons oil in a pot on medium heat; when the oil is hot, sprinkle the brown sugar evenly over the base of the pot. Let the sugar melt and when it starts to bubble, add the chicken and sear it, turning often, until browned and coated with the "burnt" sugar, about 8 minutes. Add the peas and stir. Add 1 cup of the reserved cooking liquid and the coconut milk and cook for about 30 minutes.

5 Stir in the rice and up to another cup of the reserved cooking liquid as needed and bring to a boil. Cook for about 5 minutes, then add the onions, pumpkin, carrots and Scotch bonnet. Season with salt and pepper and simmer until much of the liquid has evaporated, about 15 minutes. Cover the pot and cook until all the liquid has evaporated, 30 to 40 minutes.

6 Serve garnished with the scallions.

JERKED PORK WITH MANGO GINGER SAUCE

If there is one dish that Jamaica is well known for, it is jerk. Our jerk seasoning is delicious and spicy enough to make you stand up and say HEY! It's the real deal, not tempered down in any way, so be warned: If you can't take the heat, stay away from the jerk! For a unique kick, we add a little coffee. Also bear in mind that Scotch bonnet peppers in Jamaica are much more spicy than the habaneros or peppers available overseas, so feel free to add more if you want to "kick it up" a notch. For a more refined version of this dish, we use pork tenderloin—simply grill it (you'll need a grilltop smoker), carve it, cover it with mango ginger sauce and pop in the oven for ten minutes, although this last step is totally up to you. We like to serve this with roasted yam and roasted ripe plantains, and Creole Spiced Slaw (page 135).

Serves 10

For Our Special Super-Spicy Coffee Jerk Seasoning
(Makes about 2½ cups)
12 Scotch bonnets
½ cup vegetable oil
1 cup coconut oil
1 tablespoon molasses
1 bunch scallions, chopped
2 large cloves garlic, chopped
½ cup chopped fresh thyme
pinch of sea salt
3 tablespoons allspice berries, crushed
3 tablespoons peeled, chopped fresh ginger
1 tablespoon browning
½ teaspoon ground cinnamon
dash of freshly grated nutmeg
1 teaspoon ground coriander
2 tablespoons red rum
2 tablespoons white vinegar
¼ cup brewed coffee

5 pounds boneless pork shoulder
(or 4 pounds boneless pork tenderloin)
sea salt

For the Mango Ginger Sauce
2 cups chopped mango
1 tablespoon peeled, minced fresh ginger
2 tablespoons fresh lime juice
1 cup mango juice
2 tablespoons brown sugar
sea salt and freshly ground black pepper

Method

1 To make our special jerk seasoning, blend all the ingredients in a blender until smooth. Rub the outside of the pork with salt and place it in a baking dish. Cover with the jerk seasoning and marinate for at least 24 hours.

2 To make the mango ginger sauce, combine the mango, ginger, lime and mango juices and brown sugar in a small saucepan over medium heat and simmer for 10 minutes. Transfer to a blender and puree until very smooth. Season with salt and pepper.

3 Grill the pork on an open medium flame with a grilltop smoker, turning from time to time, for 2 hours, or until an instant-read thermometer inserted into the thickest part of the meat registers 145°F and the outside is dark and charred. Alternatively, preheat the oven to 500°F and roast the pork for 1 hour 40 minutes. Transfer the pork to a cutting board and chop into 1-inch pieces. If using boneless pork tenderloin, it will cook within 15 to 20 minutes; carve it into slices about ¼ inch thick.

4 Preheat the oven to 450°F. Place the pork in a roasting pan, ladle some mango ginger sauce over and roast for 10 minutes for the glaze to set. Serve hot, with the remaining sauce on the side.

BLUE MOUNTAIN BEEF STEW WITH STOUT

In Jamaica, "stew beef" is a popular lunch item, often served with rice and peas. In this version, we add Jamaican stout and coffee, and braise the beef instead of stewing it over the fire as is traditonal. It comes out a bit more like a beef bourguignon, which we happen to love; the stout, however, adds a much more intense flavor than red wine.

Serves 6 to 8

1 teaspoon dried rosemary
2 bunches fresh thyme, chopped
8 cloves garlic, chopped
½ inch fresh ginger, peeled and grated
½ Scotch bonnet, seeded and minced
1 teaspoon sea salt, plus more for seasoning
1 teaspoon freshly ground black pepper, plus more for seasoning
2 tablespoons plus ¼ cup brewed coffee, preferably Blue Mountain
1 tablespoon soy sauce
2½ pounds top round beef (stewing beef)
½ cup olive oil
½ cup to ¾ cup all-purpose flour
2 carrots, peeled and chopped
1 yellow onion, chopped
2 tablespoons tomato paste
2 bay leaves
½ cup Dragon stout
2 cups water
1 teaspoon sugar (optional)

Method

1 Preheat the oven to 325°F.

2 In a small bowl, stir together the rosemary, half the thyme and garlic, the ginger, Scotch bonnet, salt, pepper, the 2 tablespoons coffee and soy sauce. Season the beef well with salt and pepper, then rub the marinade all over the meat.

3 Heat the oil in a large Dutch oven over medium-high heat. Dust the beef with the flour and fry quickly in batches to brown. Transfer to a plate lined with paper towels and set aside.

4 Add the carrots, onion and the remaining garlic to the pot and sauté over medium heat until browned. Add the tomato paste and cook for 5 minutes. Add the bay leaves and remaining thyme.

5 Return the meat to the pot and add the stout. Cook for 10 to 15 minutes until reduced, then add the water and the remaining ¼ cup coffee and bring to a boil. Once boiling, cover the pot and place in the oven for about 2 hours, until the meat is tender.

6 Transfer the meat and vegetables to a deep serving dish. Skim off any excess fat from the cooking liquid and return to the stovetop. Reduce for 10 minutes over medium heat until thickened. Taste and adjust the seasoning with the sugar, if necessary. Pour the sauce over the meat and vegetables and serve.

GUYANESE PEPPERPOT

Pepperpot is Guyana's national dish—not to be confused with Jamaican pepperpot, which is a soup made from callaloo and coconut milk. Guyanese pepperpot is a stew made from all kinds of meats that are cooked down in cassareep (a sort of syrup made from cassava). Traditionally eaten on Christmas morning with a special plait bread, we often ate this stew while living in Trinidad, as we had great family friends who were Guyanese. We have since developed such a love for the flavor of cassareep that it always has a place in our pantries. Cassareep may be a little difficult to find, but if you happen to see it in a Caribbean market, make sure to buy some and try this delectable stew. Traditional pepperpot flavors the meats with orange peel, cinnamon, brown sugar and cloves. In our version, we season oxtail and stew pork and/or stew beef with thyme and garlic. Feel free to add in some of the traditional seasonings mentioned above, and use whatever combination of meats you desire.

Serves 8 to 10

½ Scotch bonnet, seeded and minced, plus 1 whole
1 head garlic, cloves peeled but left whole, plus 4 cloves, chopped
3 yellow onions, chopped
1 teaspoon soy sauce
1 tablespoon plus ¼ cup vegetable oil
sea salt and freshly ground black pepper
5 pounds oxtails
5 pounds stew pork (or stew beef or both)
¼ cup brown sugar
2 bunches scallions, chopped
1 tablespoon chopped fresh thyme
5 cups cassareep or beef stock
2½ cups water
chopped fresh parsley, for garnish
cooked rice or hardo bread, for serving

COOKING HINT

If cassareep is not available, you can still make a nice stew by adding a splash of molasses and soy sauce after caramelizing the sugar.

Method

1 Combine the minced Scotch bonnet, whole garlic cloves, a third of the onions, the soy sauce and 1 tablespoon oil in a large baking dish and season with salt and pepper. Add the meat, mix well and marinate in the refrigerator for at least 24 hours.

2 Heat the remaining ¼ cup oil in a large soup pot over medium heat. Add the brown sugar and cook until the sugar is caramelized—don't allow it to burn! Add the pork and sear to seal in the flavors. Transfer to a plate and set aside. Add the oxtail to the pot and sear in batches, to brown it. Return all the oxtail to the pot and add the 4 chopped cloves of garlic, the remaining onion, the scallions, whole Scotch bonnet and thyme; stir well and cook for about 5 minutes.

3 Meanwhile, in a medium bowl, mix the cassareep with the water. Gradually add the cassareep liquid, a little at a time, until the meat is covered (you won't use it all—reserve the leftovers). Bring to a boil, then reduce the heat, cover, and simmer for 30 minutes.

4 Return the pork to the pot and add some more cassareep liquid. Cook over low heat, stirring occasionally, and gradually adding more cassareep liquid as the liquid in the pot evaporates, for about 2 hours. Slow cooking is needed to tenderize the meat and infuse the flavors. The meat should always be just covered with liquid—don't add too much. Once the meat is tender and cooked through, the gravy should be nice and thick and rich.

5 Taste to adjust the seasoning, garnish with parsley and serve with rice or hardo bread.

SPICY GARLIC "PEPPER" SHRIMP

Pepper "swims," or shrimp seasoned with chile peppers, are sold by shrimp vendors on the roadside and at stoplights in various parts of the island. Served at room temperature out of little plastic bags, they make for a tasty, quick, "smoke out of the ears" snack when journeying around Jamaica. Middle Quarters, in the parish of St. Elizabeth on the south coast, is particularly well known for its pepper swims. This is our version, which we serve hot as a main dish, with our coconut rice pilaf (page 141).

Serves 4 to 6

1 pound (16 or 20 count) fresh shrimp, in shells with heads on
2 tablespoons sea salt
2 cups vegetable oil
1 Scotch bonnet, chopped with seeds
6 cloves garlic, diced
¼ cup sliced scallions
1 teaspoon sugar

Method

1 Butterfly the shrimp and remove the veins but leave the shells and heads on. Place in a bowl and rub the shrimp with 1 tablespoon of the salt; let sit for at least 30 minutes.

2 Heat the oil in a wok or skillet over medium-high heat. In batches, add the shrimp and deep-fry for 40 to 60 seconds, then quickly remove from the oil with a slotted spoon and drain on paper towels. When all the shrimp have been deep-fried, pour the oil out of the pan, leaving just 1 tablespoon.

3 In small batches, quickly sauté the Scotch bonnet, garlic, scallions, sugar and remaining 1 tablespoon sea salt over high heat for a few seconds. Add the shrimp in batches, give it a quick toss to coat with the seasoning and remove quickly from the pan; repeat until all the shrimp are finished. Serve immediately.

WHOLE ROAST SNAPPER WITH GRILLED LIME AND MOJITO OIL

Traditional roast fish in Jamaica is roasted in a foil packet with pumpkin, okra, Scotch bonnet and seasonings. We love fresh fish with a sea salty, crispy skin, so we roast this in a high oven to get it nice and charred. The mojito oil is drizzled all over the finished fish, which we serve with grilled limes—it's fresh, clean and just divine!

Serves 4

For the Mint Lime Mojito Oil
(Makes about 2 cups)
1 cup loosely packed fresh mint leaves
½ cup fresh parsley leaves, finely chopped
2 cloves garlic, chopped
2 teaspoons sugar
2 teaspoons lime zest
1 teaspoon sea salt
½ teaspoon Scotch bonnet, seeded and minced
1 cup olive oil
3 tablespoons fresh lime juice
2 tablespoons capers, chopped (optional)
1 teaspoon freshly ground black pepper

4 fresh whole snapper (1 pound each)
4 teaspoons fresh lime juice
2 tablespoons olive oil
1 bunch fresh cilantro, chopped
1 tablespoon peeled and grated fresh ginger
1 tablespoon sea sea salt
1 bunch fresh thyme sprigs
1 lime, thinly sliced
2 or 3 slivers Scotch bonnet (optional)
freshly ground black pepper
4 limes and/or lemons, halved

Method

1 To make the mint lime mojito oil, in a mortar and pestle, muddle the mint and parsley with the garlic, sugar, lime zest, salt and Scotch bonnet. Transfer to a small bowl and add the oil, lime juice, capers, if using, and pepper; let sit in the refrigerator for a minimum of 6 hours.

2 Rub each fish with 1 teaspoon lime juice. Mix together the oil, cilantro, ginger and salt in a small bowl. Score the outside of the fish with three cuts on either side and massage the marinade into the skin, the cuts and inside the cavity of the fish. Stuff each cavity with thyme sprigs, lime slices and slivers of Scotch bonnet, if using. Generously sprinkle the outside of the fish with sea salt and pepper and let rest for 1 hour.

3 Preheat the oven to 450°F. Roast the fish for 20 minutes until the skin gets slightly charred.

4 Place the limes and/or lemons directly on the oven rack, cut sides down, until marked and slightly softened.

5 Place each fish on a serving plate and drizzle generously with the mojito oil. Garnish with the grilled citrus to squeeze onto the fish to add an incredible kick!

7

AL FRESCO CARIBBEAN

GRILL PAN AND COAL POT COOKING

In the Caribbean, we are blessed with blazingly hot days and warm, sultry nights year round. We live outdoors; we eat and drink outdoors and, while we do enjoy our homes, we love to socialize under the sun and stars. In this chapter, we share some of the most popular dishes from our off-site event menus, when we often had very little equipment to work with and were working in remote and challenging venues (like the middle of the race-course track or on a remote beach or mountain top) with no electricity, no running water and very few facilities. With our paltry equipment budget, we were compelled to develop a series of recipes around the coal pot and jerk pan,

which soon became our signature, allowing us to cook fresh on site and retain authentic island flavor in our many dishes.

Many classic island recipes are traditionally prepared outdoors on a coal pot or in a grill pan. It's common to see roadside chefs selling their specialties any time of day or night on any Caribbean island—whether it's pan chicken, jerk pork, shark and bake, doubles or corn soup, the food is always hot and always divine. We consider these recipes to be more contemporary and cleaner versions of the traditional "al fresco" preparations that can be found in the islands. So stoke up your barbie and give them a go. Bon appétit!

PIMENTO-CRUSTED BEEF TENDERLOIN WITH ISLAND CHIMICHURRI

This recipe is a stripped-down version of jerk—we separate the elements that go into jerk seasoning and recombine them with this mouthwatering version of beef tenderloin. The beef is crusted with allspice berries, similar to beef au poivre, and grilled on a traditional coal pan. When ready, it is drizzled with Scotch bonnet oil and garnished with grilled scallions. A West Indian version of chimichurri made with culantro, Scotch bonnet and lime rounds this dish off nicely. We served this up family style at a beautiful colonial house in the hills of Hanover for a rehearsal dinner organized, designed and executed by Los Angeles–based event planner to the stars Yifat Oren. It was the single most spectacular event that we have ever seen, executed or had the pleasure to work on; luckily for us, the food was a hit!

Serves 8 to 10

¼ cup whole black peppercorns
½ cup allspice berries
4 to 6 pounds tenderloin beef
1¼ cups olive oil
½ tablespoon sea salt, plus more
for seasoning
4 cloves garlic, minced, plus 1 tablespoon
chopped garlic
1 bunch fresh thyme, chopped, plus
2 tablespoons chopped
1 red onion, thickly sliced
6 portobello mushrooms, caps only, sliced
3 bunches scallions
drizzle of Scotch bonnet oil, or more
to taste (page 46)

For the Caribbean Chimichurri

1 cup chopped fresh parsley
1 cup chopped fresh cilantro
½ cup culantro or chadon beni (if not
available use 1½ cups cilantro)
½ cup chopped fresh mint
¼ cup fresh lime juice
½ teaspoon minced Scotch bonnet
5 cloves garlic, chopped
1 bay leaf
1 tablespoon sea salt
1½ cups olive oil
½ teaspoon brown sugar

Method

1 Place the peppercorns and allspice on the bottom half of a dishcloth. Fold over the top half of the cloth and crush the peppercorns and allspice seeds together by rolling over them with a bottle.

2 Rub the beef with 1 cup of the oil, the salt, the 4 cloves minced garlic and the chopped bunch of thyme, making sure the beef is well salted. Roll the tenderloin in the crushed pepper and allspice mixture to coat and press the pepper and allspice into the surface of the beef. Refrigerate for at least 2 hours.

3 To make the Caribbean chimichurri, in a food processor, combine the parsley, cilantro, culantro, mint, lime juice, Scotch bonnet, garlic, bay leaf, sea salt, oil and brown sugar. Process until well blended.

4 Heat up the grill or a grill pan over high heat. Combine the remaining ¼ cup oil, 2 tablespoons chopped thyme and 1 tablespoon chopped garlic in bowl. Season with salt and add the red onion and mushrooms; mix well. Grill the onions and mushrooms, about 10 minutes total; transfer to a plate and keep warm in the oven.

5 Add the beef to the grill and cook to desired doneness, about 15 minutes for medium. Transfer to a cutting board and let rest before carving. Place the scallions on the grill until marked, about 1 minute.

6 Carve the beef and place on a platter, garnished with the grilled scallions, onions and mushrooms. Drizzle the chimichurri and the Scotch bonnet oil over the beef; serve the remaining chimichurri on the side.

GRILLED LOBSTER WITH CHILI LIME BUTTER AND JAMAICAN FEVERGRASS SAUCE

In Jamaica, "fevergrass" is what we call lemongrass—it grows wild in certain parts of the island, but is not used in cooking. Instead, it is boiled down in water and used to make what we call a bush tea to bring down a fever. Here, we grill the lobsters and dress them with a simple chili lime butter. A tart coconut, lime and fevergrass sauce is served on the side. The combination of flavors is simply out of this world!

Serves 4

1 tablespoon olive oil
2 tablespoons chopped garlic
1 teaspoon sea salt
freshly ground black pepper
3 tablespoons chopped fresh cilantro
4 whole live lobsters (1 to 1½ pounds each), split in half, or 4 (8-ounce) lobster tails

For the Chili Lime Butter

½ pound (2 sticks) unsalted butter, at room temperature
1 bunch fresh cilantro, finely chopped
juice of 6 limes (about ¼ cup)
zest of 1 lime
1 teaspoon chili powder
sea salt

For the Fevergrass Culantro Sauce

(Makes about 1 cup)
¾ cup canned coconut milk (plus more if needed)
½ cup fresh cilantro leaves
3 tablespoons chopped tender inner stalks lemongrass (from about 2 stalks)
2 stalks scallion, coarsely chopped
¼ teaspoon lime zest
1½ tablespoons fresh lime juice
¼ Scotch bonnet, seeded and minced
1 garlic clove, peeled
sea salt and freshly ground black pepper

Method

1 Place the oil, garlic, salt, a grind of pepper and cilantro in a food processor and pulse to a paste. Rub the paste all over the insides of the lobsters and let sit in the refrigerator for at least 1 hour.

2 Meanwhile, to make the chili lime butter, in a small bowl, mix the butter, cilantro, lime juice and zest, chili powder and a pinch of salt. Set aside at room temperature.

3 To make the fevergrass culantro sauce, combine the coconut milk, cilantro, lemongrass, scallions, lime zest and juice, Scotch bonnet and garlic in a blender and puree until smooth. Thin with more coconut milk by the teaspoonful, if desired. Season with salt and pepper. This can be made 1 day ahead and kept in the fridge.

4 Heat a grill or grill pan over high heat. Grill the lobsters cut side down; after 5 minutes, turn over and spread with the chili lime butter. Cook until firm, 5 to 8 minutes. Serve with the fevergrass sauce on the side.

GRILLED RACK OF LAMB WITH GRAPEFRUIT HONEY, EGGPLANT CAPONATA AND THREE-OLIVE RELISH

When we had to create meals for plated off-site dinners, we always liked to work with rack of lamb; it is easy to grill, holds well and is easy to plate. We created this dish for a sit-down family-style wedding by the seaside for a hundred and fifty people. The bride and groom were from London and really wanted lamb, so we came up with a Mediterranean presentation that could be served with some room-temperature sides, like this olive salsa and caponata. We catered the wedding as a hurricane was descending on the island, and every second we thought we would either be blown away or drowned in rain. We were lucky; we had a windy but dry evening, and the dish was very well received!

Serves 6

2 teaspoons minced garlic
¼ teaspoon minced Scotch bonnet
1 tablespoon orange zest
2 tablespoons chopped fresh thyme
1 tablespoon chopped fresh rosemary
1 tablespoon chopped fresh mint
¼ cup extra-virgin olive oil
sea salt and freshly ground black pepper
4 (7-rib) racks of lamb, trimmed

For the Three-Olive Relish

1 cup Kalamata olives, pitted and finely chopped
1 cup green olives, pitted and finely chopped
1 cup black olives, pitteed and finely chopped
½ cup olive oil
¼ cup orange juice
2 teaspoons orange zest
1 tablespoon honey, preferably Jamaican
1 teaspoon minced Scotch bonnet
1 tablespoon chopped fresh thyme
1 tablespoon chopped fresh mint
2 tablespoons finely chopped roasted garlic
2 tablespoons minced red pepper
1 tablespoon minced red onion
sea salt and freshly ground black pepper

For the Eggplant Caponata

1½ cups vegetable oil
8 cloves garlic, peeled
pinch of dried mint
pinch of dried cilantro
pinch of sea salt
3 medium eggplants, sliced
¼ cup olive oil
½ red onion, diced
¼ cup sliced scallions

1 bell pepper, diced
½ cup raisins
¼ cup distilled white vinegar
2 tablespoons honey, preferably Jamaican
5 tablespoons chopped fresh cilantro
2 tablespoons chopped fresh mint
sea salt and freshly ground black pepper

For the Honey Glaze

¼ cup honey, preferably Jamaican
1 cup grapefruit juice
1 tablespoon brown sugar
1 tablespoon chopped fresh thyme
2 tablespoons chopped fresh mint

Method

1 In a medium bowl, combine the garlic, Scotch bonnet, orange zest, thyme, rosemary, mint and oil. Whisk until blended, then season with salt and pepper. Place the lamb racks in a baking dish and pour the marinade over, working it into the meat with your hands; adjust the seasoning, if necessary. Refrigerate for a minimum of 3 hours.

2 To make the three-olive relish, in a medium bowl, combine all the olives, the olive oil, orange juice and zest, honey, Scotch bonnet, thyme, mint, roasted garlic, red pepper and red onion. Mix well and season with salt and pepper. Refrigerate for a minimum of 3 hours; the longer this sits the better it tastes.

3 To make the eggplant caponata, preheat the oven to 400°F. In a large bowl, combine the vegetable oil, garlic, mint, cilantro and salt. Add the eggplant slices and toss until well coated. Transfer the eggplant to a baking sheet in a single layer and roast for 30 minutes, until tender. Transfer to a cutting board, let cool and roughly chop. Transfer to a large bowl and set aside.

4 Warm the olive oil in a medium sauté pan. Add the red onion, scallions, bell pepper and raisins and sauté until softened, 3 to 5 minutes. Add the vinegar and honey and cook down for 2 to 3 minutes. Stir in half the cilantro and mint and transfer to the bowl with the eggplant. Season with salt and pepper and add the rest of the cilantro and mint to the bowl. Toss well.

5 Bring the lamb to room temperature. Meanwhile, make the honey glaze: In a small saucepan, combine the honey, grapefruit juice, brown sugar, thyme and mint. Simmer over medium heat until the glaze becomes syrupy, about 10 minutes.

6 Heat a grill or grill pan over medium heat. Sprinkle the lamb with a little salt just before putting it on the grill to bring out the flavors. Grill until the outside is lightly marked, while basting with the honey glaze, about 8 minutes. If you wish, you can remove the racks of lamb from the fire before cooked completely through and finish it in a 350°F oven. The whole cooking process should not take more than 10 minutes per rack—you don't want to overcook the lamb.

7 Cut each rack into three or four cutlets of double ribs, place on serving plates, drizzle with the honey glaze and serve with dollops of the eggplant caponata and olive relish.

COCONUT SHRIMP FLAMBÉED IN RUM

This dish is a great option for last-minute entertaining, or a quick meal for one. We like to serve this over our Pumpkin Rice (page 142). We love to flambé with rum, a technique we usually do with desserts (like our Flambéed Bananas, page 166). When used in this savory recipe, it brings out the subtle sweetness of the coconut cream, which is beautifully tempered with the spice of the Scotch bonnet and the tartness of the lime.

Serves 4

1 tablespoon butter
4 stalks scallion, sliced
½ yellow onion, chopped
3 cloves garlic, chopped
1 bunch fresh thyme, chopped
½ Scotch bonnet, seeded and minced
1 pound jumbo shrimp (10 or 16 count), peeled and de-veined, with tail left on
½ tablespoon sea salt
2 teaspoons freshly ground black pepper
¼ cup red rum
¼ cup canned coconut cream
1 lime, cut into wedges
fresh cilantro leaves, for garnish

Method

1 Melt the butter in a skillet over medium heat. Add the scallions, onion, garlic, thyme, Scotch bonnet and shrimp and sauté for 5 to 8 minutes, until opaque. Season with the salt and pepper, then add the rum and light it with a flame until the rum burns off. Add the coconut cream and cook for 3 to 5 minutes to reduce the liquid a bit.

2 Transfer the shrimp and sauce to a plate, add a squeeze of lime and sprinkle with cilantro.

MICHELLE'S CHAR-GRILLED BABY-BACK RIBS GLAZED WITH MOLASSES

These ribs are off da chain! The jerk and Scotch bonnet give them kick and the glaze adds a smoky sweetness. Feel free to leave out the spice; all we know is that once we start eating these, we can't stop! Serve with our Creole Spiced Slaw (page 135) and Boiled Corn with Pimento Butter (page 140).

Serves 4 to 6

For the Molasses Glaze

3 tablespoons molasses
2 tablespoons tamari sauce
6 tablespoons hoisin sauce
¼ cup Thai sweet chili sauce
¼ cup rum
6 allspice berries
1 inch fresh ginger, peeled and sliced
2 tablespoons chopped fresh thyme
5 tablespoons honey
5 tablespoons brown sugar
1 cup orange juice
¼ cup distilled white vinegar

4 pounds baby-back or pork ribs
1 bay leaf
3 inches fresh ginger, peeled, plus
2 tablespoons peeled and grated fresh ginger
12 whole garlic cloves, plus 4 cloves garlic, chopped
1 bunch fresh thyme
1 whole Scotch bonnet
1 bunch scallions, plus 3 stalks scallion, chopped
8 allspice berries
sea salt
1 tablespoon jerk sauce
3 tablespoons hoisin sauce
1 tablespoon honey
¼ cup Asian plum sauce
1 tablespoon soy sauce
2 tablespoons sesame or peanut oil
2 tablespoons chopped fresh cilantro

Method

1 To make the molasses glaze, combine all of the ingredients in a medium saucepan. Bring to a boil, then lower the heat to a simmer and reduce for about 20 minutes, until thickened.

2 Fill a large pot (big enough to fit the ribs) with water and add the bay leaf, 3 inches ginger, garlic cloves, thyme, Scotch bonnet, whole scallions and allspice and 1 teaspoon salt. Parboil the ribs for 25 to 30 minutes, or until the bones stick out at the edges. Transfer to a platter and let cool.

3 In a large stainless-steel bowl, combine the jerk sauce, hoisin sauce, honey, plum sauce, soy sauce, sesame oil, cilantro, the 2 tablespoons grated ginger, the chopped garlic and a third of the chopped scallions. Add the ribs and coat well with the marinade. Let sit in the refrigerator for at least 2 hours but preferably overnight.

4 Bring the ribs back to room temperature before cooking. Heat a grill to medium-high heat. Grill the ribs for 20 to 30 minutes, continually turning them and basting with the glaze, until sticky and dark. Alternatively, preheat the oven to 400°F, spread the ribs on a sheet pan, drizzle with the glaze and roast for 30 to 40 minutes, continually basting with glaze.

5 Place the ribs on a platter and add the remaining chopped scallions.

COOKING HINT

We've always boiled our ribs first because it saves time later when grilling fresh for a large event. However, you can skip this step and just marinate the ribs, bring to room temperature and grill them over medium-low heat for about 1½ hours, turning them often. If you choose to roast them in the oven, it will also take about 1½ hours.

HERB-DUSTED MAHI-MAHI FILLET IN BANANA LEAVES WITH COCONUT LIME SALSA

Fresh mahi-mahi is marinated, topped with herb butter, wrapped in banana leaves and cooked on the grill. The banana leaves steam up delicious little packages of fish that are bursting with flavor. Serve with a simple fresh coconut salsa and a light coconut sauce on the side.

Serves 4

1 teaspoon chopped fresh thyme
1 teaspoon sliced scallion
1 teaspoon minced garlic
½ teaspoon sea salt
½ teaspoon freshly ground black pepper
2 teaspoons olive oil
1 tablespoon fresh lime juice, plus more for drizzling
2 pounds mahi-mahi fillets (6 to 8 ounces each)
banana leaves, cut into 10-inch squares (or aluminum foil)

For the Pimento Butter
¼ pound (1 stick) unsalted butter
2 teaspoons ground allspice
3 stalks scallion, chopped
1 teaspoon chopped fresh thyme
1 garlic clove
juice of 2 limes
½ teaspoon sea salt

For the Coconut Lime Salsa
(Makes about 1½ cups)
1½ cups grated fresh coconut or shredded unsweetened coconut
2 tablespoons fresh lime juice (from about 1½ limes)
3 tablespoons currants
2 tablespoons diced red onion
2 tablespoons chopped fresh cilantro
½ teaspoon ground cumin
½ teaspoon sea salt
2 tablespoons olive oil

For the Coconut Sauce
(Makes about 1 cup)
1 (14-ounce) can coconut milk
1 tablespoon chopped fresh thyme
1 teaspoon minced Scotch bonnet
2 teaspoons diced scallion
1 teaspoon diced onion
1 teaspoon minced garlic
sea salt and freshly ground black pepper

Method

1 In a baking dish or resealable plastic bag, combine the thyme, scallion, garlic, salt, pepper, oil and lime juice. Add the mahi-mahi and marinate in the refrigerator for about 2 hours.

2 To make the pimento butter, place the ingredients in a food processor and pulse until well combined.

3 To make the coconut lime salsa, in a small bowl, combine the coconut, lime juice, currants, red onion, cilantro, cumin, salt and oil. Set aside.

4 To make the coconut sauce, in a medium saucepan over medium heat, combine the coconut milk with the thyme, Scotch bonnet, scallion, onion and garlic and cook until slightly thickened, about 5 minutes. Season with salt and pepper.

5 Singe the banana leaves over an open flame, or blanch in a pot of boiling water and grease them with a little vegetable oil. Place 1 fish fillet inside each banana leaf square, dot with some pimento butter, add a squeeze of fresh lime and roll up each banana leaf to form a package. Heat a grill or grill pan over medium heat (alternatively, preheat the oven to 350°F), place the package seam side down and grill for 10 to 15 minutes, until cooked through.

6 Cut open the packages, place on serving plates and garnish with the coconut lime salsa. Serve the coconut sauce on the side.

GRILLED JERKED SALMON FILLET AND FRESH FRUIT SALSA

While the idea of jerk does not sound like it would work with salmon, it will surprise with how delicate the flavors are. The salmon is lightly marinated in pineapple juice, rum, pimento (allspice) and ginger, grilled to perfection, then served up on a bed of sweet potato puree and garnished with a mango papaya salsa. It is light, refreshing and a lovely change of pace for both the salmon and the jerk.

Serves 6

6 individual salmon filets (about
8 ounces each)
1 lime, cut in half
¼ cup pineapple juice
¼ cup orange juice
6 tablespoons Appleton Special rum
(or any dark rum)
1 tablespoon soy sauce
1 tablespoon chopped fresh thyme
2 tablespoons ground allspice
¼ teaspoon freshly grated nutmeg
½ teaspoon minced Scotch bonnet
1 teaspoon ground cinnamon
2 stalks scallion, minced
3 tablespoons finely chopped onion
sea salt and freshly ground black pepper

For the Tropical Fruit Salsa
(Makes about 2 cups)
1 cup peeled and diced mango
1 cup peeled, seeded and diced papaya
¼ cup diced fresh pineapple
1 teaspoon crushed red pepper flakes
juice of 2 limes
½ red pepper, diced
2 teaspoons finely diced scallion
1 tablespoon chopped fresh cilantro
sea salt and freshly ground pepper

Method

1 Rub the salmon filets with the lime halves. In a large bowl, whisk together the pineapple juice, orange juice, rum, soy sauce, thyme, allspice, nutmeg, Scotch bonnet, cinnamon, scallions, onion and salt and pepper. Add the salmon to the bowl and massage the marinade into the fillets. Cover with plastic wrap and let sit in the refrigerator for at least 2 hours, turning the fillets every 30 minutes to make sure they are coated with the marinade.

2 Meanwhile, to make the tropical fruit salsa, in a medium bowl, combine the mango, papaya, pineapple, red pepper flakes, lime juice, red pepper, scallion and cilantro and stir gently. Take care not to overmix the fruits because they will become soft and mushy. Season with salt and pepper. Refrigerate for 1 hour before serving.

3 Heat a grill or grill pan to medium heat and rub the grill rack with oil. Brush the marinade off the salmon and grill the filets for 5 to 6 minutes per side, depending on the thickness, until your desired doneness. Turn the filets only once so that they don't break apart during cooking.

4 Transfer the salmon to serving plates and spoon the fruit salsa alongside.

RED STRIPE BBQ PAN CHICKEN

This is our take on Jamaican Pan Chicken. The chicken is well marinated and basted repeatedly during grilling with our homemade Red Stripe BBQ sauce. It's spectacularly good! Feel free to use any beer you have available.

Serves 10

5 pounds chicken parts
¼ cup fresh lime juice or distilled white vinegar for washing
1 bunch scallions, chopped
3 cloves garlic, minced
1 inch fresh ginger, peeled and grated
½ Scotch bonnet, finely chopped (optional)
2 tablespoons paprika
2 tablespoons olive oil
1 bunch fresh thyme, chopped
sea salt and freshly ground black pepper

For the Red Stripe BBQ Sauce

2 cups ketchup
3 tablespoons tamari
3 tablespoons Pickapeppa sauce
⅓ cup brown sugar
3 tablespoons chopped scallion
⅓ cup distilled white vinegar
2 tablespoons peeled and grated fresh ginger
2 tablespoons Dijon mustard
2 tablespoons honey
3 garlic cloves, chopped
¼ cup chopped yellow onion
1 Scotch bonnet, seeded and minced
about 1 cup Red Stripe beer

Method

1 Wash the chicken in the lime or vinegar and rinse well under running water. In a blender, combine the scallions, garlic, ginger, Scotch bonnet, if using, paprika, oil, thyme and salt and pepper. Puree to form a thick paste. Transfer to a baking dish or resealable plastic bag and add the chicken, tossing to coat. Season with more salt and pepper and marinate in the refrigerator for 24 hours.

2 Preheat the oven to 350°F.

3 To make the barbecue sauce, in a medium saucepan, combine all of the ingredients with just ½ cup Red Stripe. Simmer for about 10 minutes, stirring occasionally, until thickened and reduced. Toward the end of the cooking time, add the rest of the Red Stripe (about ¼ to ½ cup). Divide the sauce between two bowls.

4 Heat a charcoal or gas grill to medium-high heat. Dip the chicken in one bowl of the BBQ sauce and grill for about 30 minutes, continually turning the chicken and basting with the sauce throughout. Transfer the chicken pieces to a baking dish. Pour the BBQ sauce from the second bowl over the chicken pieces to coat them well.

5 Preheat the oven to 375°F. Roast the chicken in the oven for 15 to 20 minutes, until the sauce is nice and sticky and the chicken is cooked through, measuring 165°F on a meat thermometer.

6 Serve immediately.

GRILLED CHICKEN WITH SPICY WEST INDIAN SALSA VERDE

This has to be our best-loved chicken dish. The well-seasoned chicken also gets a "post-cooking" marinade; it is tossed in a bit of West Indian salsa verde and put in the oven for a few minutes so the salsa verde flavors can be absorbed into the chicken. The combo of the chargrill, the island seasonings and the kick of the West Indian salsa verde is truly unforgettable.

Serves 8 to 10

¼ cup olive oil
1 bunch scallions, sliced
8 cloves garlic
2 tablespoons peeled and grated fresh ginger
1 bunch fresh thyme
1 bunch fresh cilantro
½ Scotch bonnet, seeded and minced
¼ cup fresh lime juice (from about 6 limes)
sea salt and freshly ground black pepper
4 pounds mixed chicken parts

For the Spicy West Indian Salsa Verde
(Makes about 2½ cups)
1 cup chopped fresh parsley
⅓ cup chopped fresh chadon beni (culantro) or cilantro
1 tablespoon roughly chopped garlic
½ cup chopped scallions
1 bunch fresh thyme, chopped
1½ cups olive oil
½ cup water
6 tablespoons fresh lime juice (from about 8 limes)
2 teaspoons lime zest
1 Scotch bonnet, cut in half and seeded
1 tablespoon sea salt
1 tablespoon peeled and chopped fresh ginger

Method

1 In a blender, combine the oil, scallions, garlic, ginger, thyme, cilantro, Scotch bonnet, lime juice and salt and pepper and puree. Transfer to a baking dish or resealable plastic bag and add the chicken, tossing to coat. Marinate in the refrigerator for 12 hours or overnight.

2 Preheat the oven to 350°F.

3 To make the spicy West Indian salsa verde, in a food processor or blender, combine the parsley, chadon beni, garlic, scallions, thyme, oil, water, lime juice, lime zest, Scotch bonnet, salt and ginger. Blend well.

4 Heat a grill or grill pan to medium-high heat. Grill the chicken for about 10 minutes per side, turning once, until the outside is charred. Transfer the chicken to a baking dish and toss with the salsa verde, saving some for garnish. Bake for 10 to 15 minutes, until the chicken is cooked through and an instant-read thermometer registers 165°F. Transfer the chicken to a platter, drizzle with more salsa verde and serve.

OUR ROOTS

GROUND PROVISIONS, SIDE DISHES AND VEGGIES

Sides and vegetables are rooted, yes, in the ground—but also in our history. Many Caribbean staples like yam, sweet potatoes, cassava, dasheen, coco, plantain and green banana are inherited from our roots as a slave society. The mainstays of the slave diet were the starchy vegetables and ground provisions that provided energy and stamina for the long hours of back-breaking labor on a sugar plantation. Slaves were able to harvest many of these items for themselves. This reliance on root vegetables, along with one-pot dishes and the introduction of rice, has shaped many of the traditional meals that we still eat in the Caribbean today.

The modern Caribbean diet continues to incorporate many of these starchy vegetables as accompaniments to small amounts of protein in our daily meals. We love ground provisions, not only because of their superior nutritional value, but also for the diversity of their flavors and textures, which allows for variety at the dinner table and inspires great creativity. In this chapter, we share long time favorites along with new, innovative side dishes with Caribbean flair.

SWEET POTATO GRATIN

There is nothing that can adequately express how yummy this dish is! This is our kind of comfort food— just give it a try. We like to serve it with Mummy's roast pork (page 82) or our jerked pork (page 100). Also it's a perfect holiday side dish at Thanksgiving or Christmas dinner.

Serves 6 to 8

2 pounds sweet potatoes, peeled and cut into cubes
3 cups heavy cream
¼ cup chopped scallions
½ yellow onion, chopped
½ teaspoon chopped fresh thyme
½ Scotch bonnet, seeded and minced
4 cloves garlic, finely chopped
sea salt and freshly ground black pepper
1 cup grated Parmesan cheese
½ cup panko (Japanese) breadcrumbs

Method

1 Preheat the oven to 350°F.

2 Bring a large pot of salted water to a boil over high heat. Add the sweet potatoes and boil for 20 to 25 minutes until cooked through.

3 Meanwhile, in a small saucepan, combine the heavy cream, scallions, onion, thyme, Scotch bonnet and garlic, bring to a boil and then let simmer for 10 minutes.

4 When the sweet potatoes are soft, drain and transfer to a large mixing bowl; mash until smooth. Pour in the cream mixture, season to taste with salt and pepper and stir in half of the Parmesan. Transfer to a baking dish and top with the remaining Parmesan and the breadcrumbs. Bake for 35 minutes, until the cheese and breadcrumbs are golden brown. Serve immediately.

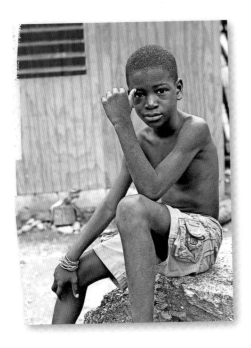

SMASHED YAM

In Jamaica, a yam is very different from what they call "yams" in the US; our yams are more dense and hearty. The yam was originally imported from Africa, and this starchy, nutrient-rich vegetable became the preferred food of slaves working the Caribbean plantations. It is also the food of champions: When Jamaican gold medalist Usain Bolt was asked what the source of his speed was, after breaking his first world record for the 100- and 200-meter sprints, he replied that it's all in the yams. Traditionally, yam was roasted over an open flame or boiled in salted water. Here, we use the yam to make a supremely satisfying casserole.

Serves 10 to 12

2½ pounds yellow yam, peeled and cubed
2 tablespoons butter
1 tablespoon minced onion
1 teaspoon minced garlic
1 stalk scallion, minced
2 teaspoons chopped fresh thyme
2 teaspoons all-purpose flour
1 cup milk
1 cup heavy cream
¼ cup white wine
sea salt and freshly ground pepper
½ cup grated Cheddar cheese
½ cup grated Parmesan cheese

Method

1 Preheat the oven to 350°F. Butter a baking dish.

2 Bring a large pot of salted water to a boil over medium-high heat. Add the yam and boil until soft, 25 to 30 minutes. Drain.

3 Meanwhile, melt the butter in a saucepan over medium heat. Add the onion, garlic, scallion and thyme and cook until the vegetables are wilted. Stir in the flour and cook for about 2 minutes, until the flour is no longer raw. Gradually pour in the milk and cream in small amounts, whisking continually, until the sauce thickens. Add the white wine, season with salt and pepper and remove the sauce from the heat.

4 Transfer the cooked yam to a large bowl and mash with a fork, leaving it quite lumpy. Add the cream sauce along with half of the Cheddar and mix well. Season with salt and pepper. Place in the prepared baking dish and sprinkle with the rest of the Cheddar and the Parmesan. Bake for 35 minutes, until nice and bubbly. Serve immediately.

INGREDIENT NOTE

Many varieties of this root vegetable are available in Jamaica—yellow yam, yampee, white yam—and they are all delicious and incredibly nutritious. Try shopping at a Caribbean store and asking for one of these varieties or you can substitute taro root.

SWEET POTATO PUREE WITH TOASTED PECANS AND BROWN SUGAR

Here is another tasty recipe for this popular starch, which mixes citric tastes with a creamy puree and tops it off with brown sugar and toasted pecans. It is a great side dish for the holiday season.

Serves 10 to 12

5 pounds sweet potatoes, peeled and cut into cubes
2 tablespoons butter
2 cups heavy cream
1 tablespoon orange zest
½ cup orange juice
4 tablespoons brown sugar
1 teaspoon ground cinnamon
sea salt and freshly ground black pepper
½ cup raw pecans, toasted

Method

1 Preheat the oven to 350°F.

2 Bring a large pot of salted water to a boil. Add the sweet potatoes to the pot and cook for 20 to 30 minutes, until soft. Drain, transfer to a blender and puree, or mash by hand.

3 Meanwhile, in a small saucepan, melt the butter over medium heat. Add the heavy cream and orange zest and juice. Whisk in about 1 tablespoon of the brown sugar and the cinnamon and simmer until thickened, about 8 minutes.

4 Pour the cream sauce over the mashed sweet potatoes and mix to combine. Season with salt and pepper and spread in a baking dish. Sprinkle with the remaining 3 tablespoons brown sugar and the pecans and bake for 35 to 40 minutes, until the top is crusty. Serve immediately.

RUM BROWN SUGAR PLANTAINS

Plantain is served as a side dish at almost every meal in the islands. In Jamaica, we eat it both ripe and green, but most often it is sliced ripe and fried in a little vegetable oil. Here, we slow bake it in guava, brown sugar and cinnamon until caramelized and golden. It's great with curries or any kind of meat.

Serves 6 to 8

¼ cup dark rum
¼ cup brown sugar
1½ cups guava juice (or any available fruit juice)
1 teaspoon ground cinnamon
¼ teaspoon freshly grated nutmeg
½ teaspoon ground allspice
3 tablespoons honey
6 large ripe plantains, peeled
3 tablespoons butter, cut into small pieces
orange zest, for garnish

Method

1 Preheat the oven to 400°F.

2 In a medium bowl, whisk together the rum, brown sugar, guava juice, cinnamon, nutmeg, allspice and honey. Place the plantains in a small roasting pan, pour the sauce over the top, and dot the tops with the butter. Roast the plantains for about 40 minutes, turning and basting them frequently. Lower the heat to 325°F and roast for another 35 minutes, or until the sauce has reduced and become syrupy and the plantains are soft.

3 Transfer the plantains to a platter and slice on the bias. Pour any sauce remaining in the pan over the top, garnish with orange zest and serve.

ROASTED MIXED POTATOES

Simple, easy and satisfying, this dish is the perfect complement to any roast. These potatoes rock with our Marmalade-Glazed Leg of Lamb (page 86)!

Serves 8

2 pounds sweet potatoes, peeled and cut into cubes

2 pounds baking potatoes, peeled and cut into cubes

¼ cup olive oil

sea salt and freshly ground black pepper

4 cloves garlic, sliced

2 tablespoons fresh rosemary leaves

2 tablespoons fresh thyme leaves

Method

1 Preheat the oven to 400°F.

2 In a large bowl, toss the potatoes with the oil, salt and pepper, garlic, rosemary and thyme; let sit for 15 minutes to allow the flavors to develop.

3 Spread out the potatoes in a thin layer on a baking sheet and roast for 15 minutes, until brown and crispy. Lower the heat to 350°F and roast until cooked through. Serve hot.

TRINI CORN PIE

One of the Trinidadian dishes we love most is corn pie. At large family meals, almost every home will have this side dish, which is more like a corn pudding, made with both corn kernels and creamed corn.

Serves 6

½ cup canned corn kernels, liquid reserved

1 large egg, at room temperature

½ teaspoon sea salt

½ teaspoon freshly ground white pepper

8 tablespoons finely ground cornmeal

4 tablespoons salted butter, plus more for greasing

¾ cup chopped onions

¾ cup chopped bell peppers

½ Scotch bonnet, seeded and minced, or to taste

2 cups canned evaporated milk

2 tablespoons chopped fresh cilantro

½ cup creamed corn

1 cup grated sharp Cheddar cheese

Method

1 Preheat the oven to 350°F. Grease a baking dish with butter.

2 Pour the reserved corn kernel liquid into a measuring cup. If the liquid does not fill 1 cup, add enough lukewarm water to bring it up. Pour the liquid and egg into a large bowl. Add the salt and white pepper and beat to mix well. Add the cornmeal and stir to form a smooth paste. Set aside.

3 Melt the butter in a medium saucepan over medium heat. Add the onions, bell peppers and Scotch bonnet and sauté until the onions are translucent. Pour in the evaporated milk and bring the mixture to a boil. Immediately stir in the cornmeal paste and reduce the heat to low; cook for 4 minutes, stirring intermittently.

4 Stir in the whole corn. Cook on low heat until the mixture comes away easily from the sides of the pot, about 5 minutes.

5 Remove the pot from the heat and stir in the cilantro, creamed corn and ½ cup of the cheese. Transfer to the prepared baking dish, smooth the surface and sprinkle the remaining ½ cup cheese on top. Bake for 30 minutes, or until the cheese is melted and golden brown.

6 Let rest for at least 30 minutes before cutting and serving.

TWICE-ROASTED LOCAL MIXED VEGETABLES

This vegetable dish is bursting with so many wonderful flavors and textures that it will blow your mind! Your friends and family are sure to keep coming back for more. We like to serve this alongside the Grilled Chicken with Spicy West Indian Salsa Verde (page 122).

Serves 4 to 6

5 plum tomatoes, quartered
4 to 5 cloves garlic
2 onions, quartered
2 tablespoons plus ¼ cup olive oil
1 bunch fresh rosemary, chopped
1 bunch fresh thyme, chopped
sea salt and freshly ground black pepper
1½ ripe plantains, cut into cubes
3 carrots, peeled and cut into cubes
2 red and yellow peppers, cut into cubes
2 cho cho (chayote), peeled and cut into cubes
1 cup string beans, trimmed
2 cups cauliflower florets
2 cups peeled and cubed calabaza pumpkin

Method

1 Preheat the oven to 400°F.

2 In a large baking dish, toss the tomatoes, garlic cloves and onions with the 2 tablespoons oil and half the rosemary and thyme. Season with salt and pepper and roast for 20 minutes, until all the vegetables are soft and the tomatoes have released their juices. Remove from the oven and toss well so that tomato juice coats all the vegetables.

3 In a large bowl, combine the plantains, carrots, red and yellow peppers, cho cho, string beans, cauliflower and pumpkin. Season with a generous quantity of salt, the remaining herbs and the remaining ¼ cup oil. Add the uncooked vegetable mixture to the tomato, onion and garlic mixture and toss to combine. Roast for another 20 to 25 minutes, until all the vegetables are cooked through but still firm. Serve hot.

CHO CHO PACKETS

Inspired by a delicious recipe from Jamie Oliver, we decided to try cho cho a new way and roast-steam them in these delightful packets of flavor. These would be a great accompaniment to our whole roast snapper (page 107) or grilled jerked salmon (page 120).

Serves 6 to 8

6 cho cho (chayote), peeled and sliced
½ cup white wine
1 bunch fresh thyme
sea salt and freshly ground black pepper
5 tablespoons salted butter, cut into pieces

Method

1 Preheat the oven to 350°F.

2 Place a large square of foil on a baking sheet and fold up the sides. Add the cho cho and pour the white wine over the top. Add the thyme and season with salt and pepper. Dot with the butter and close up the foil to make a packet. Roast for 35 minutes, until the cho cho is tender.

3 Cut open the foil package and serve hot.

CREOLE-SPICED SLAW

We made this dish for a fabulous island-themed rehearsal dinner that we catered in the Hamptons for our great friend, television personality Robyn Moreno. None of the guests was from the Caribbean, although we did have a few Tejanos and they simply loved the island flava! This cool summer slaw is spicy-sweet perfection with any kind of barbeque—from burgers to ribs to chicken. Enjoy!

Serves 6

For the Sweet and Spicy Jerked Cashews
1¼ cups raw cashews
2 teaspoons jerk sauce
sea salt
1 tablespoon butter
3 tablespoons brown sugar

For the Coconut Sesame Dressing
juice of 6 limes (about 6 tablespoons)
1 stalk lemongrass, tender inner part only, smashed and finely chopped
1 stalk scallion, chopped
2 tablespoons honey, preferably Jamaican
1 tablespoon brown sugar
2 tablespoons dark Asian sesame oil
1 teaspoon soy sauce
¼ teaspoon minced Scotch bonnet
¼ cup canned coconut milk

6 ounces white cabbage, thinly shredded (2 to 3 cups)
6 ounces red cabbage, thinly shredded (2 to 3 cups)
½ medium red pepper, cut into matchsticks
½ medium yellow pepper, cut into matchsticks
1 red chile pepper, seeded and finely sliced into strips
½ red onion, thinly sliced
½ cup thinly sliced strips fresh pineapple
1 ripe mango, peeled, pitted and cut into thin strips
1 medium ripe papaya, peeled and cut into thin strips
sea salt and freshly ground black pepper
1 bunch fresh mint, chopped
1 bunch fresh cilantro, chopped
toasted grated coconut (optional)

Method

1 To make the sweet and spicy jerked cashews, preheat the oven to 350°F. In a small bowl, toss the cashews with the jerk sauce and a little salt. Spread on a baking sheet in a single layer and toast until golden, about 5 minutes.

2 Melt the butter in a saucepan over medium heat. Add the brown sugar and let melt; when it begins to caramelize, add the roasted cashews and toss to coat well. Spread the cashews out onto a baking sheet lined with waxed paper to cool. Roughly chop.

3 To make the coconut sesame dressing, in a blender, combine all of the ingredients and whizz together. Season with salt and pepper.

4 In a large bowl, combine both cabbages, all the peppers, the red onion, pineapple, mango and papaya. Season with salt and pepper. Pour the dressing over the vegetable and fruit mixture, add the mint and cilantro and toss. Top with the sweet and spicy cashews and toasted coconut, if using. Serve chilled.

ROASTED PUMPKIN AND FIGS WITH LIME TAHINI

Michelle was obsessed with this dish when she lived in Fort Greene, Brooklyn, and had access to the farmers' market. When figs came into season, it was all she wanted—the bright mint paired with the tang of the lime tahini, the sweetness of the pumpkin and figs, and the crisp of the roasted garlic! Add spice to the tahini by throwing in some slivered Thai green chiles. It makes a great dipping sauce, too.

Serves 6

4 pounds pumpkin, peeled and chopped
8 fresh figs, quartered
½ red onion, sliced
8 cloves garlic
¼ cup olive oil
1 bunch fresh mint, chopped
sea salt and freshly ground black pepper
Chadon Beni Oil (page 46)

For the Lime Tahini

juice of 2 limes
1 teaspoon honey
¼ cup hot water, plus more if needed
¼ cup tahini
1 teaspoon peeled and grated fresh ginger
2 tablespoons chopped fresh mint
1 tablespoon chopped fresh cilantro

Method

1 Preheat the oven to 400°F. On a large baking sheet, toss the pumpkin, figs, red onion and garlic cloves with the oil. Sprinkle with the mint and season well with salt and pepper. Roast for about 20 minutes, or until caramelized.

2 Meanwhile, to make the lime tahini, in a small bowl, whisk together the lime juice, honey, hot water and tahini. Add the ginger, mint and cilantro. Season with salt and pepper and thin with a little more water or some olive oil as needed.

3 Assemble the roasted vegetables on a platter. Drizzle with the tahini sauce and chadon beni oil just before serving.

STRING BEANS WITH GINGER AND GARLIC

String beans are one of the few vegetables that you can always get at the local market here, and we always try to stay local. Finding delicious and creative ways to prepare them has always been a challenge. This dish is extremely simple, but very tasty and goes with just about any kind of protein!

Serves 6 to 8

1½ to 2 pounds string beans, trimmed
1 tablespoon salted butter
1 tablespoon olive oil
4 cloves garlic, minced
1 inch fresh ginger, peeled and minced
1 bunch fresh thyme, chopped
1 bunch fresh mint, chopped
sea salt and freshly ground black pepper

Method

1 Blanch the string beans in a large pot of boiling salted water for about 5 minutes, until bright green. Transfer to a colander and immediately run under cold water to stop the cooking process. Don't overcook the beans; they should be bright and fresh in color, with a crunch.

2 Melt the butter and oil in a sauté pan over medium heat. Add the garlic and ginger and cook until golden brown and crispy, but be careful not to let them burn! Add the thyme and mint, then quickly toss in the string beans. Season with salt and pepper and serve.

INGREDIENT NOTE

If you live in the United
States, feel free to swap in
ripe plantains or sweet potatoes,
which are not as dense as pumpkin but work
really well too. Any other kind of squash or
starchy vegetable can also be substituted.

TWICE-FRIED PRESSED GREEN PLANTAIN WITH AVOCADO, CILANTRO AND MANCHEGO

This easy snack is an unexpectedly delectable treat. As simple as it looks, you will be utterly but pleasantly surprised by the burst of flavors that awaken your taste buds as you bite into the hot plantain. Your guests will not be able to stop talking about it—if there's actually any left for them, that is.

Serves 8

2 large green plantains
about 3 cups vegetable or coconut oil
sea salt and freshly ground black pepper
1 large avocado, pitted and sliced
1 bunch scallions, chopped
2 tablespoons fresh lime juice, or to taste
4 ounces Manchego cheese, grated (about 1 cup)
1 bunch chopped fresh cilantro
¼ cup Spicy West Indian Salsa Verde (page 122)

Method

1 Cut off both ends of each plantain and, with the tip of a paring knife, score lengthwise along the ridges of the plantain skin; peel away the skin. Cut the plantains into 2-inch-thick pieces and sprinkle with salt.

2 Heat about 4 inches oil in a large pot over high heat. Once the oil is very hot, drop the plantain pieces into the oil and fry for about 2 minutes. Transfer the plantains to a plate lined with paper towels to drain. Reserve the oil in the pot.

3 Spread a clean dish cloth on a work surface, place 1 piece of fried plantain on the cloth, and fold the cloth over the plantain; press hard with the heel of your hand to flatten the plantain to about ½ inch thick. Repeat with the remaining pieces of plantain. Once all the plantains are pressed, heat the oil up again and fry the plantains for 3 minutes more, or until golden brown. Transfer to a plate lined with fresh paper towels to drain. Season with salt.

4 In a small bowl, mash together the avocado with the scallions, a pinch of salt and the lime juice.

5 Place some mashed avocado on top of each pressed plantain and top with cheese, cilantro and a generous drizzle of spicy salsa verde. Serve immediately.

MAMA'S BANANA FRITTERS

Our grandmother, Mama, made these with her leftover overripe bananas at the end of the week and served them with her meatloaf and rice and peas. We'd steal them from the kitchen and munch away without her ever knowing we were there—we're smooth like that! Serve as a side dish or tasty snack.

Serves 10

6 overripe bananas
2 teaspoons vanilla extract
¼ teaspoon freshly grated nutmeg
1 cup all-purpose flour
½ cup whole milk or water
3 tablespoons vegetable oil
½ teaspoon ground cinnamon
2 tablespoons sugar

Method

1 In a large bowl, mash the bananas with a fork until they form a smooth, wet puree; you should have about 1 cup. Mix in the vanilla and nutmeg. Add the flour and a touch of milk and mix to thoroughly combine.

2 Heat the oil in a large frying pan over medium heat. Drop tablespoonfuls of the banana mixture into the oil and fry until golden on one side. Flip over and fry for 2 minutes more. Transfer to paper towels to drain.

3 Mix the cinnamon and sugar together and sprinkle over the hot fritters.

GREEN BANANAS STEWED IN COCONUT MILK

We ate this dish for the first time when we were teenagers, at the country home of a well-known Jamaican artist, Judy Ann Macmillan, in St. Ann—and we have never forgotten it. The green bananas were stewed in a Dutch oven over an outdoor fire and served with an array of barbequed meats. It was one of the simplest and most memorable meals we have ever had—authentic Jamaican country cooking.

Serves 4

2 stalks scallion, finely chopped
¼ yellow onion, finely chopped
¼ Scotch bonnet, seeded and finely chopped
1 bunch fresh thyme, finely chopped
2 cups canned coconut milk
2 cups water
1 bay leaf
1 teaspoon sea salt
12 medium green bananas, peeled and quartered (see page 148)
freshly ground black pepper

Method

1 In a small bowl, combine the scallion, onion, Scotch bonnet and thyme.

2 In a saucepan, bring the coconut milk, water, bay leaf, thyme and salt to a boil. Add the onion mixture and bananas to the pot and return to a boil. Reduce the heat and simmer for about 1 hour, until the coconut milk forms a custard.

3 Divide among 4 bowls, grind some fresh pepper over the top and serve.

BOILED CORN WITH PIMENTO BUTTER AND CHEESE

When Michelle lived in Fort Greene, Brooklyn, every Saturday she would head to the Fort Greene Flea Market to browse, chill a bit, buy a donut (or six) from Dough and eat corn on the cob rolled in chile and sprinkled with Mexican cheese. This is our ode to that dish, but we've added a little "Yardie," or Jamaican, flavor.

Serves 6

12 cups water
1 pound (4 sticks) butter
1 bunch scallions
4 cloves garlic
6 Scotch bonnets
2 tablespoons sea salt
1 bunch fresh thyme
6 allspice berries
2 bay leaves
6 ears corn, husks reserved
4 ounces Pimento Butter (page 119)
4 ounces Asiago cheese, grated (about 1 cup)
Spiced Salt (page 55), to taste
3 fresh limes
3 tablespoons chopped fresh cilantro

Method

1 In a large pot, combine the water, butter, scallions, garlic, Scotch bonnets, salt, thyme, allspice and bay leaves. Bring to a boil, add the corn and boil until the corn is very tender, about 45 minutes (less if using fresh American corn).

2 With tongs, remove the corn from the water. Roll each corn cob first in the pimento butter, then in the cheese, then return the cobs to their husks. Garnish each corn cob with some Spiced Salt, a squeeze of fresh lime juice and the cilantro. Serve immediately.

COCONUT JASMINE FRIED RICE PILAF WITH CASHEWS AND RAISINS

The sweetness of the raisins combined with the crunch of the cashews add complexity to the flavor and texture of this rice pilaf. This is outstanding with garlic or coconut shrimp (pages 104 or 115).

Serves 10

2 cups water
1 (14-ounce) can coconut milk
2 teaspoons sea salt, plus more for seasoning
1 pound jasmine rice
2 tablespoons coconut oil
½ onion, chopped
2 tablespoons chopped garlic
1 teaspoon peeled and grated ginger
2 stalks scallion, chopped
2 tablespoons chopped fresh thyme
zest of ½ lime
1 teaspoon minced Scotch bonnet
½ cup raisins
1 cup cashews, toasted
freshly ground black pepper
2 tablespoons chopped fresh cilantro

Method

1 In a large pot, combine the water, coconut milk and salt and bring to a boil. Add the rice, lower the heat to low and cook, covered, for 25 minutes.

2 Heat half of the oil in a sauté pan, and add half of the onion, garlic, ginger, scallions, thyme, lime zest, Scotch bonnet, raisins and cashews. Sauté for 3 to 5 minutes over medium heat, until the onions are transluscent; season with salt and pepper. Add half of the rice and toss together. Transfer to a large bowl and repeat with the remaining ingredients.

3 Sprinkle the cilantro on top and serve.

RICE AND PEAS (OR GUNGO PEAS)

All islands have some version of rice and peas, and every island chef has his own recipe or way of making it; here's ours! We always use dried peas when making this except during Christmastime when fresh gungo, or pigeon, peas are available (see the Cooking Hint at right).

Serves 12

2 cups dried red peas or dried pigeon peas (see Cooking Hint)
5 cups cold water
3 cloves garlic
1 (14-ounce) can coconut milk
1 inch fresh ginger, peeled and grated
3 to 4 stalks scallion, chopped
1 bunch fresh thyme, chopped
1 whole Scotch bonnet
6 allspice berries
1 tablespoon sea salt
freshly ground black pepper
1½ pounds long-grain rice

Method

1 In a large bowl, add the peas to the cold water and soak overnight.

2 Tranfer the peas and soaking water to a large pot, add the garlic and bring to a boil. Lower the heat and simmer for 40 minutes, or until the peas are cooked. Add the coconut milk, ginger, scallions, thyme, Scotch bonnet, allspice, salt and a few grinds of pepper. Simmer for 20 minutes, reduce the heat to low, add the rice and stir once. Cover and cook for another 30 minutes until all the water is absorbed. Remove the whole Scotch bonnet and serve.

Variation: For a quick rice and peas using canned beans, bring 2 cups cold water to a boil with all the seasonings, coconut milk and drained canned peas. Stir in the rice and bring to a boil, reduce the heat, cover and simmer for 30 minutes until the liquid is evaporated.

PUMPKIN RICE

We love pumpkin rice—when the flavors in the dish meld together, it is a magical experience. It makes a great side dish, but is also good enough to be eaten as a meal on its own!

Serves 12

1 pound calabaza pumpkin, roughly chopped
1 tablespoon olive oil
1 stalk scallion, chopped
½ yellow onion, chopped
3 cloves garlic, chopped
1 bunch fresh thyme, chopped
1 teaspoon sea salt
½ teaspoon freshly ground black pepper
3 cups hot water
1 (14-ounce) can coconut milk
2 bay leaves
1 whole Scotch bonnet
1 pound rice, preferably basmati or jasmine
2 tablespoons butter

Method

1 Chop half of the pumpkin into a fine dice; leave the remainder in a chunky chop.

2 Warm the oil in a sauté pan over medium heat. Add the scallion, onion and garlic and cook for 2 to 3 minutes. Add the pumpkin, thyme, salt and pepper and sauté for about 5 minutes. Add the hot water, coconut milk, bay leaves and Scotch bonnet and bring to a boil. Gently stir in the rice and return to a boil. Add the butter, reduce the heat to low, cover and simmer for 30 minutes, until the rice is cooked and all the liquid has been absorbed. Carefully remove the whole Scotch bonnet and serve.

COOKING HINT

If you are using fresh gungo peas, simmer them in 3 cups water with all the seasonings and the coconut milk for about 20 minutes. Add the rice, cover and simmer for another 30 minutes until cooked. Total cooking time is 50 minutes.

9

RISE AND SHINE
BREAKFAST AND BRUNCH

Every morning when we were kids, with annoying regularity, our father would wake us up for school by turning on the lights and shouting at the top of his lungs: "Rise and shine, rise and shine!" But now we know, he just wanted to make sure we had time to eat a healthy breakfast before school. Breakfast is important family time; memories of morning meals spent with our grandparents and at home still linger.

Michelle was a porridge baby; Suzanne hated eggs. Here, we share recipes re-created from our fondest breakfast memories—morning meals from Norbrook Road in Kingston to Nutmeg Avenue in Port of Spain and everywhere else in between. These flavors from our childhood still influence our breakfast favorites to this day, and often show up on event menus and on our breakfast tables at home.

CAFÉ BELLA'S BRIOCHE FRENCH TOAST

The best French toast is made with brioche bread; its slightly sweet flavor and light texture make it fluffy, yummy and très chic. We like to top our French toast with bananas and Nutella, but feel free to substitute your fruit of choice and the more standard maple syrup instead. This was a favorite brunch item at our restaurant, Café Bella.

Serves 4

2 tablespoons coconut milk
¼ cup milk
1 large egg
2 teaspoons vanilla extract
dash of freshly grated nutmeg
4 tablespoons butter
4 thick slices brioche bread
1 large banana, sliced
4 teaspoons Nutella (or other hazelnut-chocolate spread)
1 tablespoon confectioners' sugar

Method

1 In a medium bowl, combine the coconut milk, milk, egg, vanilla and nutmeg and whisk until well combined.

2 Melt 1 tablespoon butter in a frying pan over medium heat. One piece at a time, soak the bread in the milk mixture and cook until browned on both sides, about 2 minutes per side. Transfer to a plate and keep warm. Add another tablespoon butter to the pan and repeat with another piece of bread until all four slices are browned.

3 Top each slice of French toast with sliced bananas, 1 teaspoon Nutella and a dusting of confectioners' sugar.

NUTTY GRANOLA

One of our favorite ways to start the day is with creamy yogurt, homemade granola, the crunch of nuts and the sweetness of fresh fruit and a drizzle of honey. If you love granola as much as we do, try this version, which is cooked low and slow for 1½ hours.

Serves 12

4 cups rolled oats
½ cup roasted almonds
½ cup sea salted cashews
½ cup shelled pistachios
1 cup grated fresh coconut or shredded unsweetened coconut
¼ cup brown sugar
2 tablespoons honey
¼ cup olive oil
1 teaspoon sea salt
1 cup raisins
½ cup sliced dried apricots

Method

1 Preheat the oven to 250°F.

2 In a large bowl, combine the oats, almonds, cashews, pistachios, coconut, and brown sugar. In another bowl, mix the honey, oil and salt. Pour the wet mixture onto the dry mixture and stir to coat, then spread out on two sheet pans.

3 Bake for 1½ hours, making sure to turn the granola with a spatula every 15 minutes or so to ensure an even toasty color. Transfer to a large bowl, then mix in the raisins and apricots. Store in an airtight container for up to 2 weeks.

GENIE'S CORNMEAL PORRIDGE WITH COCONUT AND BAY LEAF

Traditionally in Jamaica, porridge is breakfast food—a tradition most likely inherited from the wave of Scottish migrants that came to Jamaica in the early 1900s. Our great grandfather, McAllister, was one among them. Porridge is often the go-to food for "pickney" (Jamaican speak for kids or children) and babies. Country folks say that porridge babies are strong, healthy and "traptin" (strapping)! We particularly love this version, which Imogene Brown (aka Genie) used to make for us and our catering team for breakfast on those eternally long workdays that started before dawn. We added a couple bay leaves for a subtly different flavor that is simply delicious.

Serves 6

4 cups water, plus more for thinning

3 cups freshly made coconut milk (see page 24), or 1 (14-ounce) can coconut milk mixed with 1 cup water

2 bay leaves

1½ cups fine cornmeal

¼ teaspoon sea salt

2 teaspoons vanilla extract

½ nutmeg seed, freshly grated

½ cup brown sugar

¾ cup sweetened condensed milk, or to taste (optional)

Method

1 In a large pot, bring 3 cups water and the coconut milk to a boil along with the bay leaves.

2 Meanwhile, in a small bowl, mix the cornmeal with 1 cup of water so that the cornmeal does not become lumpy when added to the coconut milk mixture. Once the coconut milk is boiling, add the salt, then pour in the cornmeal mixture and start whisking right away. Lower the heat to medium-low and continue whisking so that the cornmeal does not get lumpy. Reduce the heat to low and simmer for another 20 minutes, whisking every 2 minutes or so. If the porridge gets too thick, add more water as needed.

3 When ready to serve, remove the bay leaves and add the vanilla, nutmeg, brown sugar and, if desired, condensed milk to taste.

COOKING TIP

The key to making a good Jamaican porridge is the inclusion of both nutmeg and vanilla. It's also very important not to have a lumpy porridge, so stir well and consistently to avoid any lumps!

HYACINTH'S GREEN BANANA PORRIDGE

In Jamaica, we love porridge so much that we turn everything we can into porridge—cornmeal, hominy corn, peanut, cashew, green plantain, oats, you name it! We particularly love Hyacinth's green banana porridge; the addition of oats makes for a hearty and healthy meal. This is island-style comfort food at its best. It makes a great (albeit different) supper on a cold winter's night!

Serves 8

6 medium-green small bananas, peeled (see Cooking Note)
2 tablespoons all-purpose flour
2 tablespoons oats
1 cup milk
1 quart water
1 packet coconut milk powder mixed with 2 tablespoons water
2 teaspoons vanilla extract
dash of freshly grated nutmeg
dash of ground cinnamon
pinch of sea salt
2 tablespoons brown sugar, or to taste
2 tablespoons sweetened condensed milk, or to taste (optional)

Method

1 Grate the bananas on a hand-held grater into a bowl (or you could finely chop them in a food processor). Mix in the flour, oats and milk.

2 In the meantime, bring the water to a boil in a heavy-bottomed saucepan. Add the banana mixture and, stirring constantly so that it doesn't get lumpy, return the mixture to a boil.

3 Reduce the heat to medium or low and simmer, continuing to stir for about 10 minutes so that the porridge doesn't develop lumps. Once it has thickened a bit, and the mixture has begun to cook (you will see it come together), stir in the coconut milk, vanilla, nutmeg, cinnamon and salt. Bring to boil while stirring, then turn the heat all the way down to low, cover and simmer without stirring for 35 to 40 minutes.

4 Remove from the heat and mix in the brown sugar and condensed milk, if using; taste and adjust the seasoning, adding more vanilla, coconut milk, cow's milk or nutmeg as desired. The porridge should be thick and smooth. Serve piping hot!

COOKING NOTE

Before peeling the green bananas, rub 1 teaspoon vegetable oil on your hands (or alternatively, you could peel the bananas under running water); the bananas are very starchy and your hands will become sticky. Place a bowl of water near your cutting board; you'll add the peeled bananas to the water so that they don't turn brown. Cut off the stem end of a banana. Score a deep cut down the side of the banana with the tip of the knife, then cut off the other end of the banana. Peel off the skin using your hands and use the edge of the knife to scrape away any excess strings of skin. Place in the bowl of water until ready to cook. Repeat with the other bananas.

TRINI-STYLE SALT FISH AND BAKE

All of our islands cook salt fish (salt cod) in one way or another for breakfast, lunch and even dinner. As our childhood years were spent in Trinidad, we favor this Trini version, known there as "buljol." Salt fish is often served alongside some kind of fried dumpling, some fluffy and large, others smaller and dense. In Jamaica, we serve salt fish with johnnycakes, small, round fried dumplings. Other countries, like Trinidad and Guyana, call them "bake," and they are usually the size of a small pita bread. Here, we pair this traditional Trini salt fish with our version of a bake—a hybrid recipe inspired by the bakes served in Trinidad, Guyana and Belize. If you have any left over, these little breads are also great topped with Cheddar cheese and guava jam, or even just butter and jam.

Serves 6 to 8

For the Trini-Style Salt Fish
2 cups salt fish, boiled, picked and cleaned (see page 24)
½ cup chopped tomato
½ cup chopped onion
1 Scotch bonnet, seeded and minced
¼ cup olive oil
¼ cup chopped fresh cilantro
sea salt and freshly ground black pepper

For Our Version of Bake
2 cups all-purpose flour, plus more for rolling
1½ teaspoons baking powder
1 teaspoon sea salt
1½ teaspoons butter, cut into pieces
¼ cup water
5 tablespoons plus 1 teaspoon whole milk
2 cups vegetable oil

Method

1 To make the salt fish, in a small heatproof bowl, combine the salt fish with the tomato, onion and Scotch bonnet. Heat the oil in a small pan over high heat. When very hot, pour the oil over the salt fish mixture. Add the cilantro and season with sea salt and pepper. Let rest at room temperature for about 1 hour.

2 To make our version of bake, in a fine-mesh sieve, sift together the flour, baking powder and salt into a medium bowl. Using your hands, rub the butter into the flour until well combined. Gradually add the water and milk and mix well with your hands until a dough is formed. Turn out onto a floured work surface and knead for about 5 minutes or until smooth.

3 Roll the dough into golf ball–size pieces (you should get about 8 total) and let rest for about 30 minutes.

4 Heat the oil in a large pot over high heat. Roll each dough ball out to a 4-inch disk and score a line in the middle so that it cooks more quickly. Working in batches, fry the disks in the oil for about 2 minutes, turning over once. When the bake floats, it is ready. Place on a plate lined with paper towels to drain.

5 Serve the warm bakes with the salt fish. Refrigerate any leftover buljol for up to 2 days.

ACKEE AND BACON QUICHE

In this dish, we combine a traditional quiche custard with pure Jamaican love by adding our national fruit (and popular breakfast item), ackee, alongside crispy bacon. Throw in tons of flavor from the Scotch bonnet, scallion, tomato, garlic, thyme and Parmesan cheese, and you have a winning brunch. If you don't have coconut milk on hand, use 1½ cups heavy cream instead of the cow's and coconut milk.

Makes 1 (8-inch) quiche (serves 6 to 8)

For the Quiche Crust and Custard
½ pound (2 sticks) chilled butter, cut into pieces
1 pound all-purpose flour, plus more for rolling
pinch of sea salt
up to ¼ cup ice water
1 cup whole milk
½ cup canned coconut milk
3 large eggs
1 tablespoon Dijon mustard
dash of freshly grated nutmeg
sea salt

For the Ackee and Bacon Filling
2 tablespoons olive oil
2 tablespoons chopped yellow onion
½ Scotch bonnet, seeded and minced
2 cloves garlic, minced
1 (8-ounce) package bacon, finely chopped
2 tablespoons sliced scallion
1 bunch fresh thyme, chopped
¼ cup finely chopped tomato
2 tablespoons finely chopped bell pepper
1 (18-ounce) can ackee
sea salt and freshly ground black pepper
1 cup freshly grated Parmesan cheese

Method

1 Preheat the oven to 350°F.

2 To make the quiche crust, combine the butter, flour and salt in a bowl with your hands until crumbly. Add just enough ice water to form a dough and knead until it comes together. Form into a ball, then, on a floured surface, roll the dough into a round about 14 inches in diameter. Transfer to an 8-inch quiche pan and press the dough gently into the bottom and sides. Weigh down the dough with raw rice on a piece of waxed paper and parbake for 20 minutes. Set on wire rack to cool until ready to fill.

3 Meanwhile, to make the custard, in a medium bowl, combine the milk, coconut milk, eggs, mustard and nutmeg and whisk together thoroughly. Season with salt pepper. Set aside until ready to bake.

4 To make the filling, heat the oil in a frying pan over medium heat. Toss in the onion, Scotch bonnet and garlic and cook for about 5 minutes, until softened. Add the bacon and sauté for about 5 minutes. Spoon off the excess fat and stir in the scallion, thyme, tomato and bell pepper; cook another 5 minutes or until the vegetables are tender. Add the ackee, season with salt and pepper, and mix in the Parmesan. Let cool.

5 To assemble the quiche, place the ackee and bacon filling in the pastry shell and smooth the top. Pour the custard over the filling, distributing it evenly with a fork. Return the quiche to the oven and bake for 45 minutes, or until the custard has set. Cool slightly before serving.

SMOKED MARLIN AND SALMON PLATTER WITH DILL CREAM CHEESE, LIME AND HARD-BOILED EGGS

A simple and sophisticated breakfast, brunch or lunch favorite, this lovely platter features smoked marlin, capers, marinated onions, dill cream cheese and boiled eggs. Accompany it with a baguette, bagels or our local toasted hardo bread and "you gone clear" (you can't go wrong), as we say in Jamaica!

Serves 6

Dill Cream Cheese Blend (page 56)
3 ounces smoked marlin (or smoked trout), thinly sliced
3 ounces smoked salmon or gravlax, thinly sliced
6 hard-boiled eggs, peeled
Onion-Caper Relish (page 56)
2 limes, sliced
freshly ground black pepper
6 toasted or fresh bagels, baguette or, our favorite, toasted hardo bread

Method

1 Mound the cream cheese blend in the middle of a platter, layer the marlin on one side and the salmon on the other. Halve the eggs and place around the edge of the platter.

2 Sprinkle the onion relish all over the salmon and marlin and scatter some lime slices on top. Sprinkle some pepper over all the ingredients on the platter and serve with the bagels on the side.

PAN-ROASTED PUMPKIN, BACON AND GOAT CHEESE FRITTATA

Bursting with goodness, this frittata made even Suzanne, who hates eggs, go crazy! We love roasted pumpkin and goat cheese, especially when it's warm and soft. Throw in some bacon, and it's a downright love affair of flavors for the palate! If calabaza pumpkin is not easy to find, feel free to use butternut squash.

Serves 4 to 6

1 tablespoon olive oil
½ (8-ounce) package bacon, finely chopped
½ onion, chopped
1 clove garlic, diced
2 tablespoons chopped fresh thyme
1 pound calabaza pumpkin, peeled and cut into ⅛-inch-thick slices
6 to 8 large eggs
1 teaspoon sea salt, plus more for seasoning
¼ teaspoon freshly ground black pepper, plus more for seasoning
2 ounces chèvre (or other soft goat cheese)
¼ cup grated Parmesan cheese

Method

1 Preheat the oven to broil, with a rack set 3 to 4 inches from the broiler.

2 Place a 10-inch nonstick ovenproof sauté pan over medium heat. Add the oil and bacon and sauté until browned.

3 Transfer the bacon to a plate and set aside. Pour off most of the bacon fat into a small bowl and return the pan to the heat. Add the onion, garlic, and half of the thyme, sauté for 2 to 3 minutes, then add the pumpkin. Season with salt and pepper and sauté for about 5 minutes, adding more bacon fat if the pan gets too dry. Place the pan in the oven and cook, uncovered, for about 15 minutes, until the pumpkin is soft.

4 In the meantime, whisk the eggs in a large bowl and add the remaining thyme, salt and pepper. Combine half of the goat cheese and Parmesan and whisk into the eggs.

5 Remove the pan from the oven, pour the egg mixture in and stir with a spatula to make sure the egg gets underneath the pumpkin. Dot the top with the remaining goat cheese and cook over medium heat, without stirring, until the egg mixture has set on the bottom and begins to set on top, about 4 minutes.

6 Sprinkle the top with the remaining Parmesan. Put the pan underneath the broiler until the egg mixture is lightly browned and puffy, 3 to 4 minutes. Loosen the frittata from the pan by moving a rubber spatula around the edges. Slide the frittata onto a plate or other serving dish, and cut into 6 wedges. Serve warm or at room temperature.

SWEET FOR MY SWEET

DESSERTS AND SUGARY SNACKS

There is a great reggae song, the first line of which says: "Sweet for my sweet and sugar for my honey," perfectly summing up the Jamaican love of all things sweet. Jamaica's dessert culture is a distinct blend of our British colonial influences (evidenced in the prevalence of puddings, buns and tarts) and more rustic preparations that are a product of our slave legacy. These indigenous desserts often combine basic ingredients like coconut, ginger, flour and sugar, as more expensive ingredients would not have been available to the average yeoman.

Coconut drops, peanut cake, grater cake, jack-ass corn (a traditional thin and crispy biscuit), Bustamante backbone (a gingery coconut hard candy), along with sweet potato, cassava and cornmeal pone are all examples of typical sweets inherited from our slave ancestors; all are still sold and consumed around the island to this day. In this chapter, we share recipes for a range of simple kitchen desserts, candies and baked goods that we feel aptly reflect the diversity of Caribbean desserts.

MANGA'S BREAD PUDDING

Manga, our paternal grandmother, was the baker of the family, and boy, could she bake! From puddings, to Easter buns, to patties and plantain tarts, she could do it all. She was well known for her bread pudding and we would often beg her to make us this treat whenever we visited; we modernize her family recipe by adding a coconut and rum crème anglaise. This is also delicious served warm served with rum and raisin ice cream (page 164).

Serves 10

12 large eggs
1 quart whole milk
½ cup rum
½ teaspoon sea salt
2 teaspoons vanilla extract
2 teaspoons almond extract
4 teaspoons sugar
1 whole loaf Jamaican hardo bread, cut into 1-inch cubes
½ cup raisins
4 teaspoons ground cinnamon
¼ pound (1 stick) unsalted butter, melted
Coconut Rum Crème Anglaise, for serving (page 160)

Method

1 Preheat the oven to 350°F.

2 In a large bowl, whisk the eggs, milk, rum, salt, vanilla and almond extracts and 2 teaspoons of the sugar in a bowl until the sugar is dissolved.

3 Place the cubed bread in a baking dish. Scatter with the raisins and sprinkle with 2 teaspoons of the cinnamon. Pour the milk mixture over the bread, then pour the melted butter on top. Sprinkle the top of the bread pudding with the remaining 2 teaspoons cinnamon and 2 teaspoons sugar.

4 Bake for 45 minutes until the pudding is set. Serve warm with the crème anglaise alongside.

CHOCOLATE COFFEE BREAD PUDDING

Coffee—especially Jamaica's own Blue Mountain coffee—and chocolate make perfect partners in a luscious bread pudding that we have served with great aplomb at Bellefield Great House in Montego Bay to rave reviews, over and over again.

Serves 12

12 large eggs

3 cups whole milk

1 cup very strong brewed coffee

2 tablespoons rum

2 teaspoons vanilla extract

½ teaspoon sea salt

1½ cups plus 2 teaspoons sugar

1 whole loaf Jamaican hardo bread, cut into 1-inch cubes

2 ounces good-quality white baking chocolate, roughly chopped

2 ounces good-quality semisweet chocolate, roughly chopped

4 teaspoons ground cinnamon

1 cup chocolate chips

¼ pound (1 stick) butter, melted

3 tablespoons slivered almonds

Method

1 Preheat the oven to 350°F.

2 In a medium bowl, whisk together the eggs, milk, coffee, rum, vanilla, salt and 1½ cups sugar until the sugar is dissolved.

3 Place the cubed bread in a baking dish. Scatter the white and semisweet chocolate pieces over the bread cubes; sprinkle with 2 teaspoons of the cinnamon.

4 Melt the chocolate chips in a saucepan over low heat. Drizzle the melted chocolate over the bread. Pour the coffee and milk mixture on top, then the butter. Sprinkle the top of the bread pudding with the remaining 2 teaspoons cinnamon, 2 teaspoons sugar and the slivered almonds.

5 Bake for 45 minutes until the pudding is set. Serve warm.

MATRIMONY AMBROSIA

Matrimony is a Jamaican dessert that, as its name implies, is the marriage of two outstandingly distinctive fruits: the star apple, a milky purple fruit with a star at its center when it's halved, and the most wonderful Jamaican orange, the ortanique, which is a hybrid of the tangerine and the navel orange. These two lovers are united by a bond of condensed milk in the traditional recipe for a match made in heaven. In our version, we make this divine pairing even more celestial by using a coconut rum crème anglaise instead.

Serves 8

For the Coconut Rum Crème Anglaise
2 cups heavy cream
2 tablespoons red rum
½ cup coconut milk powder
1½ cups confectioners' sugar
¼ cup canned coconut milk

2 cups ortanique or Valencia orange segments (from about 4 ortaniques)
2 cups peeled, cubed star apples (from about 4 star apples) or 1 cup each cubed pineapple and mango
1 cup freshly grated coconut or shredded unsweetened coconut
1 cup pecans, toasted and chopped

Method

1 To make the crème anglaise, in the bowl of a stand mixer fitted with the whisk, mix the heavy cream, rum, coconut milk powder and confectioners' sugar and beat until stiff peaks form. Whisk in the coconut milk.

2 Combine the ortanique segments, star apples and grated coconut in a mixing bowl. Stir in the crème anglaise. Transfer to a glass serving bowl, top with the pecans, cover with plastic wrap and refrigerate for 2 hours before serving.

TÍA MARIA TIRAMISU

Tía Maria, a Jamaican coffee-based liqueur, and moist sponge cake are the highlights of this cool island-style tiramisu. One-third Tía Maria to two-thirds milk makes a delicious cocktail called a Brown Cow that we loved ordering at Devon House back in the day. We encourage you to try both the tiramisu and the Brown Cow; they are delightful creations for all coffee lovers.

Serves 12

5 egg yolks
1¼ cups sugar
1 teaspoon plus 1 tablespoon vanilla extract
1 pound mascarpone cheese
2 cups heavy cream
1 cup coconut milk powder
¼ cup rum
1½ cups chilled brewed coffee, preferably Blue Mountain
⅓ cup Tía Maria (coffee liqueur)
1 (6-inch) ready-made sponge cake, sliced
4 ounces semisweet chocolate, shaved

Method

1 Put the egg yolks in a mixing bowl and set it over a double boiler. Add ¼ cup of the sugar and the 1 teaspoon vanilla and whisk until the yolks start to turn pale yellow. Cook over simmering water, scraping the sides of the bowl occasionally with a rubber spatula, until thick. Cover with plastic wrap and refrigerate until cool.

2 Place the cheese in a bowl and stir until smooth.

3 In the bowl of a stand mixer fitted with a whisk, combine the heavy cream, coconut milk powder, the remaining 1 cup sugar and the rum and whip until not quite stiff. Add the softened mascarpone and the chilled egg yolk mixture and fold gently together with a rubber spatula. Cover with plastic wrap and refrigerate for 1 hour.

4 In another bowl, combine the coffee, Tía Maria and remaining 1 tablespoon vanilla. Arrange the slices of sponge cake in a single layer in a 9 x 13-inch baking pan. Spoon a small amount of the coffee mixture over the cake. Plop a third of the coconut cream mixture on top and spread it into an even layer. Cover with a layer of shaved chocolate. Repeat the process two more times, until you've used all the coffee mixture, coconut cream and shaved chocolate. Cover the pan with plastic wrap and refrigerate for at least 2 hours before serving.

DALTON'S PLANTAIN TARTS

Dalton is our amazing chef at Bellefield Great House in Montego Bay, and he has a wealth of experience, good vibes and good food. His recipe, which we share here, for the typical Jamaican sweet treat, plantain tarts, is sensational! We fold the pastry like a turnover, enclosing the traditionally red-colored filling of very ripe sweet plantains.

Makes 12 hand pies

For the Pastry

1 pound all-purpose flour
1 teaspoon sea salt
½ pound (2 sticks) cold butter, cut into ½-inch pieces
up to 4 tablespoons ice-cold water

For the Filling

3 very ripe (black) plantains
¼ cup granulated sugar
2 teaspoons vanilla extract
1 teaspoon freshly grated nutmeg
2 teaspoons red food coloring
1 egg white, beaten
¼ cup confectioners' sugar, for dusting

Method

1 To make the pastry, sift the flour and salt into a medium bowl. Using your hands, rub in the butter until well incorporated and the mixture appears sandy in texture. Stir in the water until a dough forms, then knead on a work surface for a few turns to bring the dough together. Tightly wrap the dough in plastic, and chill for 3 hours in the refrigerator.

2 Meanwhile, to make the filling, peel the plantains and cut into pieces. Place in a small saucepan with enough water to cover and bring to a boil, then simmer until tender, 5 to 10 minutes, depending on how ripe the plantains are. Once soft, pour out the water, and mash the plantains with the granulated sugar, vanilla, nutmeg, and food coloring. Set aside to cool.

3 When ready to bake, preheat the oven to 350°F.

4 Roll out the dough on a lightly floured surface to about ¼ inch thick. Cut the dough into a dozen 4- or 5-inch circles. Spoon a little of the plantain filling into the center of each circle, then fold in half to form a crescent shape. Press the edges together with a fork and place the pies on a baking sheet. Slice a small hole in the top of each pie to act as an air vent, brush with the egg white, and sprinkle with the confectioners' sugar. Bake for 20 to 25 minutes, until golden brown.

5 Let the pies cool to room temperature before serving.

COCONUT DROPS

On a recent visit to New Orleans for Michelle's presentation on traditional Jamaican sweets and Jamaican candy ladies at the New Orleans's Historic Collection and Dillard University, we met Leah Chase the chef/owner of New Orleans's Dooky Chase Restaurant (the first African American–owned fine dining restaurant in America). She said her grandmother explained that pralines were originally made with coconut before they were made with pecans. All of our traditional Jamaican candies are made with coconut and, no doubt, these similarities are not a coincidence, but date back to the shared heritage of slavery, African ancestors and the plantation systems in both the Caribbean islands and the American South. Here is our recipe for coconut drops, which are made with just four basic ingredients. Give 'em a try—they are easy and tasty!

Makes 12 to 16 drops

1 medium dried coconut
5 to 6 tablespoons peeled, minced ginger
2 cups water
3 cups dark brown sugar

Method

1 Using a hammer, break the coconut and remove the hard outer shell. Using a small knife, dice the hard coconut flesh into small cubes. (You should have about 1½ cups chopped coconut.)

2 Combine the coconut and ginger in a bowl, then place in a saucepan. Add the water and brown sugar to the coconut and bring to a boil over high heat.

3 Reduce the heat to medium and cook, stirring frequently, for 1 hour 45 minutes to 2 hours, until the water has evaporated and the sugar is caramelized and sticky.

4 Place a large banana leaf or a sheet of greased waxed paper on the kitchen counter. Drop spoonfuls of the mixture on the banana leaf and let them cool and harden before serving. These keep for up to 1 week.

HOMEMADE ICE CREAM

Rum and raisin, coconut, coffee and stout are, without a doubt, the bestselling flavors for Jamaican ice cream. Jamaican rum and raisin ice cream is distinctive because we have fantastic rum; the same can be said for our local coffee ice cream. In Jamaica, you'll also find a wide range of atypical ice cream flavors: sour sop, guava, grape nut, prune, fruit and nut, pineapple and mango are all regularly available and in demand on Sundays, which is "ice cream day" for many families across the island. The recipes that follow are reminiscent in flavor to our infamous Devon House Ice Cream in Kingston.

RUM AND RAISIN ICE CREAM

Makes about 1 pint

½ cup sugar, or less to taste
1 tablespoon plus 1 teaspoon cornstarch
⅛ teaspoon sea salt
1¾ cups canned evaporated milk
1 cup heavy cream
1 egg yolk
1½ teaspoons vanilla extract
½ cup red rum
¼ cup raisins

Method

1 Combine the sugar, cornstarch and salt in a large heavy saucepan. Gradually whisk in the evaporated milk and heavy cream over medium heat and cook for 10 to 12 minutes, stirring constantly, or until the mixture thickens slightly. Remove from the heat.

2 Whisk the egg yolk in a small bowl until slightly thickened. Temper the yolk by gradually whisking about 1 cup of the hot cream mixture into the yolk, then add the yolk mixture to the remaining cream mixture in the saucepan, whisking constantly. Whisk in the vanilla and ¼ cup of the rum. Cool for 1 hour, stirring occasionally.

3 Place plastic wrap directly on the surface of the cream mixture, and chill for 8 to 24 hours.

4 Soak the raisins in the remaining ¼ cup rum and refrigerate for at least 3 hours or overnight. Drain any excess liquid from the raisins and stir the raisins into the chilled cream mixture.

5 Pour the mixture into the container of a 1½-quart electric ice cream maker, and freeze according to manufacturer's instructions.

COCONUT ICE CREAM

Makes about 1 pint

½ cup sugar
1 tablespoon plus 1 teaspoon cornstarch
⅛ teaspoon sea salt
2 cups canned coconut milk
1 cup heavy cream
1 egg yolk
1½ teaspoons vanilla extract
¼ cup shredded unsweetened coconut (optional)

Method

1 Combine the sugar, cornstarch and salt in a large heavy saucepan. Gradually whisk in the coconut milk and heavy cream and cook over medium heat, stirring constantly, for 10 to 12 minutes, or until the mixture thickens slightly. Remove from the heat.

2 Whisk the egg yolk in a small bowl until slightly thickened. Temper the yolk by gradually whisking about 1 cup of the hot cream mixture into the yolk, then add the yolk mixture to the remaining cream mixture in the saucepan, whisking constantly. Stir in the vanilla and coconut, if using. Cool for 1 hour, stirring occasionally.

3 Place plastic wrap directly on the surface of the ice cream mixture, and chill for 8 to 24 hours.

4 Pour the mixture into the container of a 1½-quart electric ice cream maker, and freeze according to manufacturer's instructions.

COFFEE ICE CREAM

Makes about 1 pint

½ cup sugar
1 tablespoon plus 1 teaspoon cornstarch
⅛ teaspoon sea salt
1 cup canned evaporated milk
1 cup heavy cream
1 egg yolk
1½ teaspoons vanilla extract
1 cup extra-strong freshly brewed coffee
½ cup chocolate-covered coffee beans (optional)

Method

1 Combine the sugar, cornstarch and salt in a large heavy saucepan. Gradually whisk in the evaporated milk and heavy cream and cook over medium heat, stirring constantly, for 10 to 12 minutes, or until the mixture thickens slightly. Remove from the heat.

2 Whisk the egg yolk in a small bowl until slightly thickened. Temper the yolk by gradually whisking about 1 cup of the hot cream mixture into the egg yolk, then add the yolk mixture to the remaining cream mixture in the saucepan, whisking constantly. Stir in the vanilla and coffee and continue whisking for about 5 minutes until well combined. Cool for 1 hour, stirring occasionally.

3 Place plastic wrap directly on the surface of the ice cream mixture, and chill for 8 to 24 hours. Just before adding to the ice cream machine, stir in the coffee beans, if using.

4 Pour the mixture into the container of a 1½-quart electric ice cream maker, and freeze according to manufacturer's instructions.

STOUT ICE CREAM

Makes about 1 pint

½ cup sugar
1¼ cups stout
1 tablespoon plus 1 teaspoon cornstarch
⅛ teaspoon sea salt
1 cup evaporated milk
¾ cup heavy cream
1 egg yolk
1½ teaspoons vanilla extract

Method

1 Warm the stout over medium heat in a small saucepan. Add ¼ cup of the sugar and whisk until melted. Set aside.

2 Combine the remaining ¼ cup sugar, the cornstarch and salt in a large heavy saucepan. Gradually whisk in the evaporated milk and heavy cream over medium heat, stirring constantly, for 10 to 12 minutes, or until the mixture thickens slightly. Remove from the heat.

3 Whisk the egg yolk in a small bowl until slightly thickened. Temper the yolk by gradually whisking 1 cup of the cream mixture into the yolk. Then add the yolk and cream mixture back into the remaining cream mixture in the saucepan, whisking constantly. Whisk in the vanilla and the stout mixture. Cool for 1 hour, stirring occasionally.

4 Place plastic wrap directly on the surface of the ice cream mixture, and chill for 8 to 24 hours.

5 Pour the mixture into the container of a 1½-quart electric ice cream maker, and freeze according to manufacturer's instructions.

CREPES À LA MODE WITH FLAMBÉED BANANAS AND WARM ORTANIQUE RUM SAUCE

To flambé safely at home, make sure that you have a metal cover handy that is large enough to tightly fit your saucepan. That way if the flame becomes too large you can control the flame by cutting off the oxygen. Slightly warming the alcohol by placing it in a pot of recently boiled water will make the flame catch more quickly. Add in the scoop of ice cream (we like coconut), and this dessert is just deeevine!

Serves 8 to 10

For the Crêpes

3 large eggs
1½ cups milk
1½ tablespoons rum
1 cup all-purpose flour
½ teaspoon sea salt
6 tablespoons butter, melted

For the Flambéed Bananas

¼ cup brown sugar
3 tablespoons butter, at room temperature
½ teaspoon ground cinnamon
¼ cup ortanique or orange juice
6 bananas, sliced diagonally
¼ cup Grand Marnier or Cointreau
3 tablespoons Appleton Estate rum (or other dark rum)

¼ cup ortanique or orange juice
1 tablespoon ortanique or orange zest
10 tablespoons confectioners' sugar
9 tablespoons butter, at room temperature
3 tablespoons Appleton Estate rum (or other dark rum)
ortanique or Valencia orange segments, for serving
vanilla ice cream or Coconut Ice Cream (page 164), for serving

Method

1 To make crêpes, whisk together the eggs, milk and rum in a medium bowl. Add the flour and salt and beat until smooth—the batter should be slightly thick, but still liquid in consistency. Refrigerate for about 30 minutes or up to 2 hours.

2 To make the flambéed bananas, melt the brown sugar, butter and cinnamon in a large saucepan over medium heat until the sugar is melted and bubbling. Whisk in the ortanique juice and reduce for about 3 minutes. Add the bananas and sauté until softened and beginning to brown. Pour the Grand Marnier over the bananas and reduce until evaporated, about 2 minutes. Splash with the rum and light with a match, allowing the rum to burn off. Set aside off the heat.

3 In a medium saucepan, simmer the ortanique juice and the zest with the confectioners' sugar over medium heat until reduced by half, about 5 minutes. Whisk in the butter, a little at a time. Add the rum just before serving; in the meantime, keep warm or set aside at room temperature.

4 Heat a crêpe pan over medium heat; brush with some melted butter. Pour about 3 tablespoons batter into the pan, swirling to spread it around evenly. Cook until the bottom is golden, flip over and cook until the other side is golden, about 1 minute more. Transfer to a plate and keep warm.

5 Fill the crêpes with the flambéed bananas and roll up like a burrito. Cut diagonally in half and top with the ortanique segments and ice cream. Add the rum to the rum sauce, pour over the crêpes and serve.

CARAMELIZED BANANA AND COCONUT CRÈME BRÛLÉE

Crème brûlée is one of Michelle's favorite desserts, and this one is "nice cyant done," meaning that the niceness cannot end. The addition of coconut, banana and nutmeg gives this traditional French favorite an island twist. We have served it at various events with great success, one of which was the official dinner for HRH the Prince of Wales at Jamaica House when he visited in 2008.

Serves 6

Flambéed Bananas (see page 166)
2 cups heavy cream
1 cup coconut milk
2 teaspoons vanilla extract
1 teaspoon freshly grated nutmeg
6 egg yolks
9 tablespoons sugar

Method

1 Preheat the oven to 325°F.

2 Divide the flambéed bananas among six wide, shallow crème brûlée dishes or 6-ounce ramekins and let cool.

3 Place the heavy cream and coconut milk in a medium saucepan. Add the vanilla and nutmeg and bring the cream just to a boil, then remove from the heat and set aside.

4 Place the egg yolks and 5 tablespoons of the sugar in a stainless-steel bowl over a pan of boiling water. Whisk the egg yolks and sugar together, and then stir over the simmering water until the mixture becomes fairly thick, about 15 minutes. Add the cream mixture to the egg mixture, and continue to whisk over the double boiler for about 10 minutes until it forms a custard.

5 Ladle the custard over the cooled flambéed bananas in the six dishes. Place the dishes in a roasting pan, and fill the pan with enough hot water to come halfway up the sides of the dishes. Bake for 40 minutes, or until the custards are set in the center. Remove the dishes from the pan, and chill for at least 3 hours.

6 When you are ready to serve, sprinkle about 2 teaspoons sugar over each custard, distributing it evenly. Place the ramekins under a broiler until the sugar caramelizes, or heat with a kitchen blow torch. Serve while the crust is still hot.

EASY NO-BAKE GINGER LYCHEE TRIFLE

Trifle is a common dessert in the Caribbean during the holiday season, and is admittedly very British in origin. Because of our colonial past, many of our food influences came from the so-called mother land, and the tradition of Christmas trifle is one of them. This easy version, which uses a store-bought rum cake as its base, was inspired by an incredible trifle we ate one night at the Guilt Trip Restaurant in Kingston, and the supreme talent of its chef/owner and fellow foodie, Colin Hylton. Colin's innovative use of local fruits and ingredients in his dessert creations are nothing short of extraordinary. His culinary creations, both sweet and savory, define modern Caribbean cuisine at its most glorious.

Serves 12

2 teaspoons Bird's custard powder
1 cup coconut milk
1 cup heavy cream
3 tablespoons sugar
1 envelope powdered ginger tea
2 teaspoons peeled and grated ginger
1 small store-bought rum cake (or 1 pound cake, drizzled with rum), split horizontally into 3 layers
¼ cup ortanique or orange juice
¼ cup sliced almonds, toasted
2 ortaniques or Valencia oranges, in segments
1 (14-ounce) can lychees, sliced (liquid reserved)

For the Drunken Whipped Cream

½ cup heavy cream
2 tablespoons sugar
1 teaspoon rum

Method

1 Place the custard powder in a small bowl. Warm the coconut milk, heavy cream and sugar in a saucepan, stirring until the sugar melts. Pour the hot cream mixture over the custard powder and whisk until the custard begins to thicken. Add the powdered ginger tea and grated ginger and whisk to combine. Set aside to cool.

2 To make the drunken whipped cream, in the bowl of a stand mixer, whisk the cream, sugar and rum until stiff peaks form.

3 To assemble the trifle, place a layer of rum cake at the bottom of a glass bowl, top generously with one-third of the ginger custard, drizzle with ortanique juice and sprinkle with almonds. Add one-third of the ortanique segments and lychees, top with another layer of rum cake, pour over another third of the ginger custard and ¼ cup lychee juice and top with almonds, lychees and oranges. Add the final layer of cake, followed by the remaining third of the custard and juice and topped with the rest of the fruit. Top with the drunken whipped cream and a sprinkle of almonds. Refrigerate for at least 2 hours before serving.

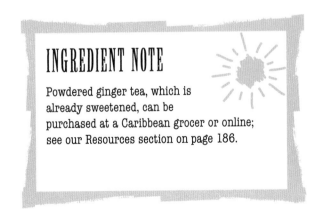

INGREDIENT NOTE

Powdered ginger tea, which is already sweetened, can be purchased at a Caribbean grocer or online; see our Resources section on page 186.

LEMON PASSION FRUIT SQUARES

Sweet yet tart and definitely "moreish," or addictive, this harmonious mixture of lemon and lime with a twist of passion fruit is, in a word, blissful! Here is our Caribbean take on the typical lemon square.

Makes 12

For the Crust

½ pound (2 sticks) unsalted butter, at room temperature
½ cup sugar
2 cups all-purpose flour
⅛ teaspoon sea salt

6 extra-large eggs, at room temperature
3 cups granulated sugar
½ cup fresh lemon juice
¼ cup fresh lime juice
2 tablespoons grated lime zest
1 cup all-purpose flour
¼ cup passion fruit pulp
confectioners' sugar, for dusting

Method

1 To make the crust, blend the butter and sugar in a stand mixer for 8 to 10 minutes, until light and fluffy. In a medium bowl, sift together the flour and salt. With the mixer on low, gradually add the flour to the butter mixture and blend until just combined.

2 Dump the dough onto a well-floured surface and gather it into a mass. Flour your hands well and use the tips of your fingers to press the dough into a 9 x 13-inch pan, building up a ½-inch edge on all sides. Chill for about 30 minutes, until the crust has set.

3 Preheat the oven to 350°F. Bake the crust for about 20 minutes, until lightly browned. Let cool completely but keep the oven on.

4 In a large bowl, whisk together the eggs, granulated sugar, lemon juice, lime juice and zest and flour. Mix in the passion fruit pulp, pour the filling over the cooled crust and bake for 40 to 50 minutes, until the filling is set. Let cool completely before dusting with confectioners' sugar, cutting into squares and serving.

BRAWTA

A LITTLE SOMETHING EXTRA

Brawta is patois for "a little something extra." For example, say you're buying fruit from a street-side fruit vendor in a very busy part of Kingston, and you want a dozen of the sweetest Bombay mangos. Because you are a good customer, the fruit vendor will give you thirteen mangos instead of twelve. The thirteenth mango is your "brawta," a little something extra from the vendor to show his or her appreciation for your patronage. (And, if you've ever tasted a Bombay mango, you would be thrilled to have an extra!) Sometimes a customer will ask for a brawta.

Probably a vestige of the old bartering system used for the exchange of goods and services, brawta is still alive and well today, especially when at the market or when buying from smaller produce vendors. So, here is our brawta for you—some special, extra recipes from our restaurant menus and many years of catering and event planning. We hope that these drinks and party snacks, decorating ideas and tips for easy entertaining will help you round out your fetin' time in true Caribbean style.

THIRST QUENCHERS: THE BASIC CARIBBEAN BAR

Whenever we think of drinks, we think of our grandfather, Hugh Holness, aka Gampi. Rum and water was his drink of choice, and we were allowed little sips at a young age to introduce our palates to the taste of fine rum. Gampi was a man who knew how to make a drink; we would bombard him with requests for a Jamaican-style ice cream soda or a Horlicks milkshake with a splash of rum and he would usually oblige. So, we dedicate this little section on the Caribbean bar to our Gampi, with whom we shared many a good drink. As he would say, "Cin cin," or cheers! If you are not into fancy cocktails or just can't be bothered to mix them, don't fret—just put our basic Caribbean bar together and let your guests serve themselves. Here is a list of what you need to get the party started. (You'll see that it is heavy on the rum!)

CARIBBEAN BAR ESSENTIALS

Red Stripe beer / Red Stripe Light (Jamaica's favorite beer)
Carib beer (Trinidad's favorite beer)
Rum cream liqueur (Wray & Nephew or Sangster's)
Angostura bitters
Tía Maria (a Jamaican coffee liquor; a good alternative is Kahlúa)
Coconut rum (try Sangster's or Wray & Nephew)
Red rum (good-quality options are Appleton, Mount Gay, Angostura and Demerrara)
White overproof rum (Wray & Nephew)
Tropical fruit juices (like guava, mango and pineapple)
Ginger ale or ginger beer
Ting (a delicious Jamaican grapefruit soda)
Shandy (you can make your own using 1 part beer to 1 part ginger ale or ginger beer)
Plenty of fresh limes
Coconut water

1-2-3-4 PUNCH: THE ONLY COCKTAIL RECIPE YOU'LL EVER NEED

We like very simple cocktails, and most times can't even be bothered to make those. But if we have to make one, we always fall back on a version of this "no fail" 1-2-3-4 punch. It's easy, quick and simple; better yet, it always works!

The recipe goes something like this:

1 of sour
2 of sweet
3 of strong
4 of weak

So, here's how it works in practice:

1 cup lemon juice or 1 part of something sour
2 cups brown sugar or 2 parts of something sweet (like honey, simple syrup or agave)
3 cups white rum or 3 parts of something strong—i.e., liquor (like vodka or red rum)
4 cups water or 4 parts of a chaser (like club soda or juice)

Mix together all the ingredients in a pitcher, pour into your glass of choice, settle back (preferably on a lounge chair) and sip away! Chill and serve over ice with a lime or orange garnish.

FETIN' 101:
HOW TO THROW AN ISLAND PARTY

In the Caribbean, we have a unique style of entertaining. Our parties are notorious for great music, crazy dancing, an abundance of food and liquor, and incredibly happy vibes. If that sounds good to you and you want to try "keeping" (Jamaican slang for hosting or throwing) a party, here is a list of simple guidelines that we always follow:

Never overplan: Last-minute fetes are always the best! We love party crashers—they bring new energy to a party and make it really swing. But, as a general rule, they should be familiar or known to you, like friends of friends. Our policy when it comes to feting is the more the merrier!

Keep it simple. Focus on the important elements: great music, easy food, plenty of liquor, lots of dancing. For larger events, make the dance floor the center focus with the bar and food surrounding it. This lets your guests see what is going on and feel the energy from the dance floor.

For a large fete, ditch the chairs and categorically no dining tables—even if you're serving food. We eat standing because we are usually dancing at the same time! If you do want to provide seating and tables, set up some casual seating away from the main party area. Sofas, outdoor benches and high-top tables informally grouped together are a great way to create less traditional dining and seating areas. Loud music is essential at a Caribbean dance party.

Have a diverse guest list. The Caribbean is known for its cultural diversity, and people of all ages always party

together. Invite that one group of people who love to dance even if they aren't your best friends. In the Caribbean we have "feting friends" who we only see when we are out, but who are great fun at a party.

Keep the liquor and food flowing!
Caribbean people have a fear of running out of anything; the drinks and party food don't have to be expensive, but it must never run out!

Warm up your guests with a strong welcome drink: our 1-2-3-4 Punch with rum (page 176) is perfect for this!

If you are having over forty guests, splurge on a bartender or two—preferably one that can dance (Caribbean bartenders always dance to the music while they serve). The rule of thumb to follow is one bartender for every twenty to thirty guests.

PARTY LINGO

In the Caribbean, we take our entertaining very seriously and have designated names for all types of events. Here are a few you will hear us throwing around a lot. All serious party people should take note.

LYME (Trini) = A casual get-together, not too large and usually thrown together at the last minute. Includes some music and dancing, or a group of people simply "lyming" (or hanging out). Also used as a verb.

FETE (Trini) = A large dance party with massive speaker boxes, a professional DJ and nonstop dancing and drinking, varying from 150 guests up to 2,000 or more. In our part of the world, fetes usually go until the sun comes up. We also have day fetes, which start at about midday and go until dark. Also used as a verb: "to fete," meaning to party. In Jamaica, a fete is referred to as a "session" or "bashment."

DANCE = A street dance party where a DJ, or "sound," sets up huge speakers outside of a bar, on the sidewalk or in the town square. The speakers usually face the road and blast dancehall music and slow jams all night long. A dance is open to all, so residents and passerbys often stop to buy a drink (stout is the drink of choice), listen to some "tunes" and "hole a cotch by a speaker box" (hang out by the speakers). From Friday evening right through to the wee hours of Monday morning, and on most public holidays (usually starting at about six p.m.), there is a dance in full swing in many communities across the island.

GET TOGETHER = Like a lyme, a small informal gathering of friends, hanging out and catching up on life; usually drinks and snacks make up the menu, with some sweet island music in the background.

MASS = Carnival Day in any island culminates with a "mass" or "road march," which is an all-day street party starting at about eight a.m. and going until dark. Revellers dress in costumes and "play mass" through the streets, "chipping," or dancing, behind music trucks that blast both live and recorded soca music at unbelievably high decibels. Copious amounts of alcohol are consumed, coupled with bacchanalian dancing. For the carnival lover, this is truly a spiritual experience!

COOK UP (Jamaican) = Cook up, or "running a boat," as we say in Jamaica, is when a group gets together to cook a meal to share. It is a form of socializing, but also a way of saving money. It is common practice on construction sites for the men to run a boat at lunchtime.

BLOCKO (Trini) = A "blocko" party hails from Trinidad and is similar to a block party in America. A road, usually in a private community, is blocked off on both ends to set up a fete. The entire street is the dance floor, and all of the required elements for a Caribbean party are in full display—DJs, loud music, gigantic speaker boxes, lots of liquor, good vibes and dancing.

THREE THINGS EVERY CATERER KNOWS

There are certain basic truths that every caterer, chef or restaurant owner knows to be self-evident. Without these truths, we would not be able to produce food for such large quantities of people with such apparent ease. Essentially, it's all about being prepared. While there are many tips that we could share, we consider these three simple pointers to be the most important in the hectic world of today—particularly if you do a lot of home cooking and entertaining.

1. Prep and Hold

Organization is, simply put, the most important aspect in hosting a successful event, no matter how large or small. Make lists, because a list can save your life. It's a sign of a great hostess, and a sign of respect for your guests, to be ready, organized and calm when you host a party. There is simply nothing worse than arriving at a dinner party to find chaos and mess; it makes you feel like you've arrived too early. A good hostess is always ready for her guests—and even if she isn't, they should never know!

In the event business, when it comes to food, we get organized by preparing all our food items to a certain point and then holding them for service. At service time (or closer to it), we "finish" the items so that the food is as fresh as possible.

Here's an example of what we would do if we had a few friends coming over for a pasta dinner:
- Prep everything and get it ready for serving:
    make the pasta sauce and hold
    grate the Parmesan

- Clean up the kitchen:

    wash everything and clean all surface mess

- Lay out all your serving utensils:

    set the table

    put on some music

    add ambiance like flowers and candles

- Get dressed and have a glass of wine while you wait for your guests! When your guests arrive, you will be relaxed and looking fabulous—and you can get your meal ready in as little as twenty minutes!

2. Batch Sauces and Dressings

One of the best ways to make sure you always have a tasty home-cooked meal is by batch preparing certain items. Many marinades, vinaigrettes, sauces and chutneys can be kept for extended periods of time (sometimes up to three weeks in the refrigerator, or more). When you make big batches of basic sauces and dressings and keep them on hand, whipping together a quick meal is easy and hassle-free.

Here are some items we are sure to have in our fridge at all times: Scotch Bonnet Oil, Spicy West Indian Salsa Verde, Coffee Jerked Seasoning, Papaya Dipping Sauce, and Peanut Coconut Dipping Sauce, to name a few, all of which are in this book! And our bonus Vinaigrette: just blend 2 cups Balsamic or red wine vinegar with 2 cups olive oil, 2 tablespoons Dijon mustard, 1 tablespoon brown sugar, 2 smashed garlic cloves, and 2 teaspoons dried rosemary. Season with sea salt and freshly ground pepper and you're good to go. These items are so tasty that they can be used with a variety of different dishes. For the home cook, batching items saves both time and money—and allows you to have a gourmet meal ready in minutes, any time at all.

3. Marinate and Portion Meat

The best thing you can do to speed up the cooking and preparation process is to prep meat in bulk, seal in individually portioned bags, date and freeze. This is not just for big dinner parties. If you live alone or have a small family, a useful tip for easy home-cooked meals in minutes is to simply marinate and portion bulk meat, poultry or fish into individual servings right after you purchase it and freeze them in separate resealable plastic bags. The portions of meat can easily be left to defrost in the fridge during the day, making dinner a few quick minutes away. And if you've followed our above advice, you should have a nice selection of fresh sauces, marinades, chutneys and salsas on hand to give your meal an extra-special twist.

SIX SIMPLE DÉCOR TIPS FOR A TABLE

We have decorated, styled and coordinated many parties during our years in the event and catering business. Over time, we have gathered some great ideas that will quickly enhance your table for any type of event with panache and ease.

- Use an eclectic mix of chairs, place settings and glassware, blending contemporary with antique pieces.
- Use colorful or patterned fabric ends to make gorgeous runners, napkins and tablecloths. Don't be afraid to mix color and patterns, as it makes a party come alive.
- Always use candles and lanterns in varying shapes and sizes to create atmosphere for evening parties. They add natural light and warmth on the dining table and throughout the party space.
- Use unique vessels and props to hold flowers, like teapots, cups and glasses.
- Try submerging tropical flowers and/or leaves in water in tall, clear glass cylinders —they are a modern and unusual alternative to typical flower arrangements in vases. Using tropical fruits in this way is also very attractive and sophisticated.
- Create different heights on your buffet table by using risers or blocks—it makes the buffet dramatic and stylish. When dressing your buffet table, create a central focus in the middle of the table—a fantastic arrangement of flowers or a piece of sculpture.

A DOZEN SUPER-EASY RECIPES FOR LAST-MINUTE ENTERTAINING

There are always going to be those times when you suddenly find yourself with unexpected visitors that you need to feed; maybe your girlfriends decide to drop by for a cup of tea or a glass of wine, and you have nothing prepared. Fear not. Here are super-easy recipes—both savory and sweet—that will get you out of any last-minute entertaining binds. All can be made in just 5 to 10 minutes. (Seriously!)

CREAM CHEESE AND PEPPER JELLY

Serves 8

1 (8-ounce) package cream cheese
½ (12-ounce) jar hot pepper jelly
1 package good-quality water crackers

Place the rectangle of cream cheese on a plate. Pour the pepper jelly over the cream cheese and let it drip down the sides. Surround with the crackers and serve.

CREAM CHEESE AND SOLOMON GUNDY DIP

Serves 8 to 10

1 package (8 ounces) cream cheese
1 teaspoon fresh lime juice
handful of chopped scallions
½ (12-ounce) jar Solomon Gundy
1 package good-quality water crackers

Blend the cream cheese, lime juice, scallions and Solomon Gundy in a food processor, or mix by hand. Transfer to a pretty bowl and serve with water crackers.

BANANA AND MANCHEGO FLATBREAD

Serves 8

2 (6- to 8-inch) readymade flatbreads or pitas
2 tablespoons banana chutney
3 ounces Manchego cheese, shaved or grated
3 tablespoons sliced black olives
sea salt and freshly ground black pepper
a handful of fresh mint leaves
2 teaspoons olive oil

Preheat your broiler. On a baking sheet, spread each flatbread with 1 tablespoon chutney, top with the cheese and olives, season with salt and pepper and sprinkle with the mint leaves. Drizzle with the oil and broil until crispy, 3 to 5 minutes. Cut each flatbread into 8 pieces and serve.

GOAT CHEESE AND PAW PAW CHUTNEY WITH CRACKERS, DRIED FRUITS AND NUTS

Serves 6 to 8

1 (8-ounce) log soft goat cheese
½ cup papaya chutney or chutney of choice
assorted dried fruits like dates and apricots
assorted nuts
assorted crackers

Place the log of cheese on a platter or cheese board. Serve with small bowls of the papaya chutney, dried fruit, nuts, and crackers.

BACON-WRAPPED PLANTAIN GLAZED WITH HONEY

Serves 6

12 (2-inch) cubes fried ripe plantain (can be made ahead and held)
6 strips bacon, cut in half
12 teaspoons honey
toothpicks

Preheat your broiler. Take the cubes of fried ripe plantain and wrap each with a strip of bacon. Secure with a toothpick and place on a baking sheet. Drizzle each plaintain with 1 teaspoon honey and broil for 5 to 8 minutes, until the bacon is caramelized and sticky. Serve immediately.

GRAPEFRUIT AND HONEY

Serves 2

1 medium grapefruit
about 2 tablespoons honey, preferably Jamaican

Cut a grapefruit in half and remove the center core with all the seeds. With a paring knife, cut out the grapefruit segments and place in two small bowls. Drizzle with the honey and serve to a surprise breakfast visitor.

BOMBAY MANGO AND ICE CREAM

Serves 2 to 4

2 Bombay mangos
4 (3-ounce) scoops Coconut Ice Cream (page 164)

Slice the mango crosswise with a sharp knife. Twist both sides in opposite directions to open the mango. Remove the pit and place both halves in bowls in the fridge to chill. Serve chilled, with a scoop of coconut ice cream in the center, for an amazing but simple dessert.

HOMEMADE ICE CREAM SANDWICHES ON GINGER SNAPS

Serves 6

6 (2-ounce) scoops of Rum and Raisin Ice Cream (page 164)
12 Jamaican ginger biscuits
¼ cup peanuts, crushed

Sandwich a scoop of ice cream between 2 ginger biscuits. Repeat with the rest of the ice cream and ginger biscuits, then roll the ice edges in the peanuts. Wrap in plastic and place in the freezer for 30 minutes before serving as a delicious snack or easy dessert for a barbeque.

BAKED BANANAS WITH CHOCOLATE AND COCONUT ICE CREAM

Serves 6

6 bananas, peeled and sliced lengthwise
1 (3½-ounce) bar milk chocolate, preferably Cadbury's, shaved
6 scoops Coconut Ice Cream (page 164) or your flavor of choice

Place each banana on a piece of foil on a baking sheet. Top with the chocolate and close up the foil to create individual packets. Bake in the oven or on the grill for 20 minutes. Open the foil and serve with a scoop of ice cream on top.

COCONUT WITH BROWN SUGAR

Serves 6 to 8

1 dry coconut, hard, fleshy insides removed (see page 24)
3 tablespoons brown sugar

Slice the firm coconut meat into thick pieces. Arrange on a platter and sprinkle with brown sugar. Serve for a great snack.

OUR MANGO CHOW

Serves 6 to 8

2 cups distilled white vinegar
1 Scotch bonnet, cut into slices, or hot pepper sauce to taste
1 teaspoon sea salt
freshly ground black pepper
½ teaspoon sugar (optional)
4 not-quite-ripe mangos, or pineapple, June plum or any firm tropical fruit, peeled and sliced

In a large bowl, stir together the vinegar, Scotch bonnet, salt, pepper and sugar, if using. Add the mango slices and macerate until the vinegar is well absorbed into the mango, about 30 minutes. Serve.

RESOURCES
SHOPPING FOR CARIBBEAN INGREDIENTS

There is a wealth of Caribbean grocery stores and supermarket chains across North America and the United Kingdom that sell all kinds of Caribbean products, making it easy to find many of the ingredients we suggest in our recipes. For our readers' shopping convenience, we have listed some of the more well-known ones below; see our website for further suggestions.

UNITED STATES

Grocery Store Chains
Publix Super Markets (across Florida)
Tropical Supermarket (Miami)
Caribbean Super Center (Orlando)
Key Food Supermarket (New York)

Online Caribbean Grocers
Grace Foods: buygracefoods.com
Jamaica Stores: jamaicastores.com
Sam's Caribbean Marketplace: sams247.com

CANADA

Grocery Stores
The Spice Centre (Edmonton, Alberta)
Caribbean Market (New Westminister, British Columbia)
Nicey's Food Mart (Toronto, Ontario)
Loblaw's Supermarkets (British Columbia, Ontario and Quebec)

Online Caribbean Grocers
Caribbean Market: caribbeanmarket.ca

UNITED KINGDOM

Grocery Stores and Markets
Authentic Jamaican Foodstore (Birmingham)
Options Supermarket (Birmingham)
Caribbean Market (London)
Brixton Market (Brixton)
Choumert Road Market (Peckham)
Tooting Market (London)

CARIBBEAN BRANDS WE REALLY LOVE

To add extra sweet island flavor to every meal, we encourage you to sample any or all of these amazing Caribbean purveyors for a wide selection of preserves, chutneys, sauces, canned goods, condiments and the best Jamaican patties you will ever eat.

Belcour Preserves: Homemade artisan preserves and chutneys made from old family recipes. The tomato chutney and mixed fruit chutney are faves of ours. belcourpreserves.com

Busha Browne: An exotic and unique selection of chutneys, pepper sauces, jams and jellies. We love the pepper jelly, banana chutney, burned orange marmalade and pukka pepper sauce. bushabrowne.com

Eaton's: A purveyor of a small selection of chutneys and preserves; they make an amazing papaya chutney that we just love, especially with goat cheese. eatonsjamaica.net

Golden Krust Patties: A well-known patty franchise in the U.S., they also serve a selection of other traditional Jamaican foods. goldenkrustbakery.com

Grace Foods: Distributes an extensive selection of Caribbean food products of all kinds—like canned ackee, coconut milk and beans—available throughout the U.S., U.K. and Canada in supermarkets and through their online stores. We love the Grace guava jelly and Grace pepper sauce (which is a bit like

Tabasco). gracefoods.com

Great House Preserves: A newer company with a small but lovely selection of jams and jellies.

Juici Beef Patties: Jamaica's other number one patty (it's a tie with Tastee Patties). juicipatties.com

Linstead Market: A small but delightful array of Jamaican canned and bottled products including canned ackee, callaloo and beans, along with a nice but small selection of preserves. We like their mango chutney and guava jam. linsteadmarketja.com

Matouk's: A Trinidadian brand that makes delicious pepper sauces, jams, chutneys and picalilly. carolinasauces.com

Pickapeppa Sauce: A must-have for any Jamaican pantry, this is known as the Jamaican steak sauce. It's made from tamarind. pickapeppa.com

Spur Tree: Another well-known brand of jerk seasoning and some preserves, including a nice guava jelly. spurtreejamaica.com

Tastee Patties: Jamaica's number one patty, available frozen for export. tasteejamaica.com

Walkerswood: Best known for their jerk seasoning and sauces. walkerswood.com

INDEX

ACKNOWLEDGMENTS

This book could never have come to life if not for the efforts, support and guidance of some very special people. We offer sincere gratitude and thanks to the following: our agent, Joy Tutela and the David Black Literary Agency, for seeing our passion and believing in our dream; our editor, Anja Schmidt and Kyle Books, for recognizing the story of Caribbean people and of our food as worthy of being told; our photographer, Ellen Silverman, for telling the stories of our lives in pictures; our food stylist, Christine Albano, for her clean eye and gifted hands on our recipes; our prop stylist, Marina Malchin, for making every setting have the right balance of sophistication and rusticity that was authentic to our vision; our friend Robyn Moreno for being our guardian angel even when she didn't know it; Uncle Pat for opening the door to the origins of the Rousseau family and how they made their way to Jamaica; Aunt Hester for allowing us to use her beautiful home and gardens; Helen and Aunty Kay for stories of Manga and the Grey/Briggs family; Aunt Cissy and Aunt Nena for their memories and information about the McAllister and Holness sides of the family; our staff, especially Petra, Sandy and Dalton; Hyacinth and Rohan for helping to keep everything in order; Alex and Jonno Edwards and Bromley for giving us a place to write along with great food and company; Rolando Prendagast and Kristal Jackson of Helium Media for their creativity, energy and inspired thinking; Natalia Welsh for coming on board at just the right time and being focused, organized and indispensable in helping us complete the manuscript; Cookie Kinkead for her quick response and the lovely photo of Norma Shirley; the indomitable Pat Ramsay; Jason and Richard Sharp of Cafe Blue and Clifton Mount Estate for their continuing loyalty, friendship and support and for never saying no; Kyle Mais and Jamaica Inn for generously accommodating us at the last minute in the midst of a very busy day; Ainsley and Marjorie Henriques and Patrick and Marguerite Lynch for being lively and patient dinner guests; Winsome and Crystal Edge for the delicious food and accommodating staff; Brian Meeks for being a great friend; John Lynch and the Jamaica Tourist Board team for their support; Gail Moaney and the Finn Partners team; Jody Staley for her spiritual guidance through thick and thin; our parents, Peter and Bev, for being supreme testers, tasters and readers; a special thanks to Liam and Jude for keeping us young at heart and for being our biggest fans.